The Poetry of Emma Lazarus
Volume 2

Emma Lazarus was born on July 22nd, 1849, in New York City, the fourth of seven children of Moses Lazarus and Esther Nathan, Sephardic Jews whose families, originally from Portugal, had settled in New York during the colonial period.

From an early age, she studied American and British literature, as well as the German, French, and Italian languages. Her early writings attracted the attention of Ralph Waldo Emerson.

Emma grew to become not only an important poet but also edited many collections of German poems, including Johann Wolfgang von Goethe and Heinrich Heine, some of which we include in these volumes.

Among her other writings are a novel and two plays in five acts, 'The Spagnoletto', a tragic verse drama and 'The Dance to Death', a dramatization of a German short story about the burning of Jews in Nordhausen during the Black Death.

Her interest in her Jewish ancestry grew markedly after reading George Eliot's 'Daniel Deronda', together with the alarming reports of the Russian pogroms following the assassination of Tsar Alexander II in 1881. As a result of this appalling anti-Semitic violence, thousands of destitute Ashkenazi Jews left Russia for New York, leading Lazarus to write articles on the subject as well as the book 'Songs of a Semite' (1882).

She began to help on a more practical level by helping to establish the Hebrew Technical Institute in New York, to provide support, resources and vocational training to help destitute Jewish immigrants become self-supporting.

Emma's best known work is "The New Colossus", a sonnet written in 1883; its lines appear on a bronze plaque in the pedestal of the Statue of Liberty placed there in 1903. It was written for and donated to an auction, conducted by the "Art Loan Fund Exhibition in Aid of the Bartholdi Pedestal Fund for the Statue of Liberty" to raise funds to build the pedestal.

In the latter part of her second trip to Europe (1885 to 1887), she fell seriously ill, it is thought with Hodgkin's lymphoma, and returned to New York City. Emma Lazarus died two months later on November 19, 1887. She is buried in Beth-Olom Cemetery in Brooklyn.

She was an important forerunner of the Zionist movement and argued for the creation of a Jewish homeland thirteen years before Theodor Herzl began to use the term Zionism.

Emma was honored by the Office of the Manhattan Borough President in March 2008 and her home on West 10th Street is included in a map of Women's Rights Historic Sites.

Index Of Poems

Afternoon

Small, shapeless drifts of cloud
Sail slowly northward in the soft-hued sky,
With blur half-tints and rolling summits bright,
By the late sun caressed; slight hazes shroud
All things afar; shineth each leaf anigh
With its own warmth and light.

O'erblown by Southland airs,
The summer landscape basks in utter peace:
In lazy streams the lazy clouds are seen;
Low hills, broad meadows, and large, clear-cut squares
Of ripening corn-fields, rippled by the breeze,
With shifting shade and sheen.

Hark! and you may not hear
A sound less soothing than the rustle cool
Of swaying leaves, the steady wiry drone
Of unseen crickets, sudden chirpings clear
Of happy birds, the tinkle of the pool,
Chafed by a single stone.

What vague, delicious dreams,
Born of this golden hour of afternoon,

And air balm-freighted, fill the soul with bliss,
Transpierced like yonder clouds with lustrous gleams,
Fantastic, brief as they, and, like them, spun
Of gilded nothingness!

All things are well with her.
'T is good to be alive, to see the light
That plays upon the grass, to feel (and sigh
With perfect pleasure) the mild breezes stir
Among the garden roses, red and white,
With whiffs of fragrancy.

There is no troublous thought,
No painful memory, no grave regret,
To mar the sweet suggestions of the hour:
The soul, at peace, reflects the peace without,
Forgetting grief as sunset skies forget
The morning's transient shower.

Admetus: To My friend, Ralph Waldo Emerson

He who could beard the lion in his lair,
To bind him for a girl, and tame the boar,
And drive these beasts before his chariot,
Might wed Alcestis. For her low brows' sake,
Her hairs' soft undulations of warm gold,
Her eyes' clear color and pure virgin mouth,
Though many would draw bow or shiver spear,
Yet none dared meet the intolerable eye,
Or lipless tusk, of lion or of boar.
This heard Admetus, King of Thessaly,
Whose broad, fat pastures spread their ample fields
Down to the sheer edge of Amphrysus' stream,
Who laughed, disdainful, at the father's pride,
That set such value on one milk-faced child.

One morning, as he rode alone and passed
Through the green twilight of Thessalian woods,
Between two pendulous branches interlocked,
As through an open casement, he descried
A goddess, as he deemed, in truth a maid.
On a low bank she fondled tenderly
A favorite hound, her floral face inclined
Above the glossy, graceful animal,
That pressed his snout against her cheek and gazed
Wistfully, with his keen, sagacious eyes.

One arm with lax embrace the neck enwreathed,
With polished roundness near the sleek, gray skin.

Admetus, fixed with wonder, dared not pass,
Intrusive on her holy innocence
And sacred girlhood, but his fretful steed
Snuffed the large air, and champed and pawed the ground;
And hearing this, the maiden raised her head.
No let or hindrance then might stop the king,
Once having looked upon those supreme eyes.
The drooping boughs disparting, forth he sped,
And then drew in his steed, to ask the path,
Like a lost traveller in an alien land.
Although each river-cloven vale, with streams
Arrowy glancing to the blue Ægean,
Each hallowed mountain, the abode of gods,
Pelion and Ossa fringed with haunted groves,
The height, spring-crowned, of dedicate Olympus,
And pleasant sun-fed vineyards, were to him
Familiar as his own face in the stream,
Nathless he paused and asked the maid what path
Might lead him from the forest. She replied,
But still he tarried, and with sportsman's praise
Admired the hound and stooped to stroke its head,
And asked her if she hunted. Nay, not she:
Her father Pelias hunted in these woods,
Where there was royal game. He knew her now,
Alcestis, and her left her with due thanks:
No goddess, but a mortal, to be won
By such a simple feat as driving boars
And lions to his chariot. What was that
To him who saw the boar of Calydon,
The sacred boar of Artemis, at bay
In the broad stagnant marsh, and sent his darts
In its tough, quivering flank, and saw its death,
Stung by sure arrows of Arcadian nymph?

To river-pastures of his flocks and herds
Admetus rode, where sweet-breathed cattle grazed,
Heifers and goats and kids, and foolish sheep
Dotted cool, spacious meadows with bent heads,
And necks' soft wool broken in yellow flakes,
Nibbling sharp-toothed the rich, thick-growing blades.
One herdsmen kept the innumerable droves
A boy yet, young as immortality
In listless posture on a vine-grown rock.
Around him huddled kids and sheep that left
The mother's udder for his nighest grass,
Which sprouted with fresh verdure where he sat.
And yet dull neighboring rustics never guessed
A god had been among them till he went,
Although with him they acted as he willed,
Renouncing shepherds' silly pranks and quips,
Because his very presence made them grave.

Amphryssius, after their translucent stream,
They called him, but Admetus knew his name,
Hyperion, god of sun and song and silver speech,
Condemned to serve a mortal for his sin
To Zeus in sending violent darts of death,
And raising hand irreverent, against
The one-eyed forgers of the thunderbolt.
For shepherd's crook he held the living rod
Of twisted serpents, later Hermes' wand.
Him sought the king, discovering soon hard by,
Idle, as one in nowise bound to time,
Watching the restless grasses blow and wave,
The sparkle of the sun upon the stream,
Regretting nothing, living with the hour:
For him, who had his light and song within,
Was naught that did not shine, and all things sang.
Admetus prayed for his celestial aid
To win Alcestis, which the god vouchsafed,
Granting with smiles, as grant all gods, who smite
With stern hand, sparing not for piteousness,
But give their gifts in gladness.

Thus the king
Led with loose rein the beasts as tame as kine,
And townsfolk thronged within the city streets,
As round a god; and mothers showed their babes,
And maidens loved the crowned intrepid youth,
And men would worship, though the very god
Who wrought the wonder dwelled unnoted nigh,
Divinely scornful of neglect or praise.
Then Pelias, seeing this would be his son,
As he had vowed, called for his wife and child.
With Anaxibia, Alcestis came,
A warm flush spreading o'er her eager face
In looking on the rider of the woods,
And knowing him her suitor and the king.

Admetus won Alcestis thus to wife,
And these with mated hearts and mutual love
Lived a life blameless, beautiful: the king
Ordaining justice in the gates; the queen,
With grateful offerings to the household gods,
Wise with the wisdom of the pure in heart.
One child she bore, Eumelus, and he throve.
Yet none the less because they sacrificed
The firstlings of their flocks and fruits and flowers,
Did trouble come; for sickness seized the king.
Alcestis watched with many-handed love,
But unavailing service, for he lay
With languid limbs, despite his ancient strength

Of sinew, and his skill with spear and sword.
His mother came, Clymene, and with her
His father, Pheres: his unconscious child
They brought him, while forlorn Alcestis sat
Discouraged, with the face of desolation.
The jealous gods would bind his mouth from speech,
And smite his vigorous frame with impotence;
And ruin with bitter ashes, worms, and dust,
The beauty of his crowned, exalted head.
He knew her presence, soon he would not know,
Nor feel her hand in his lie warm and close,
Nor care if she were near him anymore.
Exhausted with long vigils, thus the queen
Held hard and grievous thoughts, till heavy sleep
Possessed her weary senses, and she dreamed.
And even in her dream her trouble lived,
For she was praying in a barren field
To all the gods for help, when came across
The waste of air and land, from distant skies,
A spiritual voice divinely clear,
Whose unimaginable sweetness thrilled
Her aching heart with tremor of strange joy:
'Arise, Alcestis, cast away white fear.
A god dwells with you: seek, and you shall find.'
Then quiet satisfaction filled her soul
Almost akin to gladness, and she woke.
Weak as the dead, Admetus lay there still;
But she, superb with confidence, arose,
And passed beyond the mourners' curious eyes,
Seeking Amphryssius in the meadow-lands.
She found him with the godlike mien of one
Who, roused, awakens unto deeds divine:
'I come, Hyperion, with incessant tears,
To crave the life of my dear lord the king.
Pity me, for I see the future years
Widowed and laden with disastrous days.
And ye, the gods, will miss him when the fires
Upon your shrines, unfed, neglected die.
Who will pour large libations in your names,
And sacrifice with generous piety?
Silence and apathy will greet you there
Where once a splendid spirit offered praise.
Grant me this boon divine, and I will beat
With prayer at morning's gates, before they ope
Unto thy silver-hoofed and flame-eyed steeds.
Answer ere yet the irremeable stream
Be crossed: answer, O god, and save!'
She ceased,
With full throat salt with tears, and looked on him,
And with a sudden cry of awe fell prone,
For, lo! he was transmuted to a god;

The supreme aureole radiant round his brow,
Divine refulgence on his face, his eyes
Awful with splendor, and his august head
With blinding brilliance crowned by vivid flame.
Then in a voice that charmed the listening air:
'Woman, arise! I have no influence
On Death, who is the servant of the Fates.
Howbeit for thy passion and thy prayer,
The grace of thy fair womanhood and youth,
Thus godlike will I intercede for thee,
And sue the insatiate sisters for this life.
Yet hope not blindly: loth are these to change
Their purpose; neither will they freely give,
But haggling lend or sell: perchance the price
Will countervail the boon. Consider this.
Now rise and look upon me.' And she rose,
But by her stood no godhead bathed in light,
But young Amphryssius, herdsman to the king,
Benignly smiling.
Fleet as thought, the god
Fled from the glittering earth to blackest depths
Of Tartarus; and none might say he sped
On wings ambrosial, or with feet as swift
As scouring hail, or airy chariot
Borne by flame-breathing steeds ethereal;
But with a motion inconceivable
Departed and was there. Before the throne
Of Ades, first he hailed the long-sought queen,
Stolen with violent hands from grassy fields
And delicate airs of sunlit Sicily,
Pensive, gold-haired, but innocent-eyed no more
As when she laughing plucked the daffodils,
But grave as one fulfilling a strange doom.
And low at Ades' feet, wrapped in grim murk
And darkness thick, the three gray women sat,
Loose-robed and chapleted with wool and flowers,
Purple narcissi round their horrid hair.
Intent upon her task, the first one held
The slender thread that at a touch would snap;
The second weaving it with warp and woof
Into strange textures, some stained dark and foul,
Some sanguine-colored, and some black as night,
And rare ones white, or with a golden thread
Running throughout the web: the farthest hag
With glistening scissors cut her sisters' work.
To these Hyperion, but they never ceased,
Nor raised their eyes, till with soft, moderate tones,
But by their powerful persuasiveness
Commanding all to listen and obey,
He spoke, and all hell heard, and these three looked
And waited his request:

'I come, a god,
At a pure mortal queen's request, who sues
For life renewed unto her dying lord,
Admetus; and I also pray this prayer.'
'Then cease, for when hath Fate been moved by prayer?'
'But strength and upright heart should serve with you.'
'Nay, these may serve with all but Destiny.'
'I ask ye not forever to forbear,
But spare a while, a moment unto us,
A lifetime unto men.' 'The Fates swerve not
For supplications, like the pliant gods.
Have they not willed a life's thread should be cut?
With them the will is changeless as the deed.
O men! ye have not learned in all the past,
Desires are barren and tears yield no fruit.

How long will ye besiege the thrones of gods
With lamentations? When lagged Death for all
Your timorous shirking? We work not like you,
Delaying and relenting, purposeless,
With unenduring issues; but our deeds,
Forever interchained and interlocked,
Complete each other and explain themselves.'
'Ye will a life: then why not any life?'
'What care we for the king? He is not worth
These many words; indeed, we love not speech.
We care not if he live, or lose such life
As men are greedy for, filled full with hate,
Sins beneath scorn, and only lit by dreams,
Or one sane moment, or a useless hope, —
Lasting how long? the space between the green
And fading yellow of the grass they tread.'
But he withdrawing not: 'Will any life
Suffice ye for Admetus?' 'Yea,' the crones
Three times repeated. 'We know no such names
As king or queen or slave: we want but life.
Begone, and vex us in our work no more.'

With broken blessings, inarticulate joy
And tears, Alcestis thanked Hyperion,
And worshipped. Then he gently: 'Who will die,
So that the king may live?' And she: 'You ask?
Nay, who will live when life clasps hands with shame,
And death with honor? Lo, you are a god;
You cannot know the highest joy of life,
To leave it when 't is worthier to die.
His parents, kinsmen, courtiers, subjects, slaves,
For love of him myself would die, were none
Found ready; but what Greek would stand to see
A woman glorified, and falter? Once,
And only once, the gods will do this thing

In all the ages: such a man themselves
Delight to honor, holy, temperate, chaste,
With reverence for his dæmon and his god.'
Thus she triumphant to the very door
Of King Admetus' chamber. All there saw
Her ill-timed gladness with much wonderment.
But she: 'No longer mourn! The king is saved:
The Fates will spare him. Lift your voice in praise;
Sing pæans to Apollo; crown your brows
With laurel; offer thankful sacrifice!'
'O Queen, what mean these foolish words misplaced?
And what an hour is this to thank the Fates?'
'Thrice blessed be the gods! for God himself
Has sued for me, they are not stern and deaf.
Cry, and they answer: commune with your soul,
And they send counsel: weep with rainy grief,
And these will sweeten you your bitterest tears.
On one condition King Admetus lives,
And ye, on hearing, will lament no more,
Each emulous to save.' Then — for she spake
Assured, as having heard an oracle
They asked: 'What deed of ours may serve the king?'
'The Fates accept another life for his,
And one of you may die.' Smiling, she ceased.
But silence answered her. 'What! do ye thrust
Your arrows in your hearts beneath your cloaks,
Dying like Greeks, too proud to own the pang?
This ask I not. In all the populous land
But one need suffer for immortal praise.
The generous Fates have sent no pestilence,
Famine, nor war: it is as though they gave
Freely, and only make the boon more rich
By such slight payment. Now a people mourns,
And ye may change the grief to jubilee,
Filling the cities with a pleasant sound.
But as for me, what faltering words can tell
My joy, in extreme sharpness kin to pain?
A monument you have within my heart,
Wreathed with kind love and dear remembrances;
And I will pray for you before I crave
Pardon and pity for myself from God.

Your name will he the highest in the land,
Oftenest, fondest on my grateful lips,
After the name of him you die to save.
What! silent still? Since when has virtue grown
Less beautiful than indolence and ease?
Is death more terrible, more hateworthy,
More bitter than dishonor? Will ye live
On shame? Chew and find sweet its poisoned fruits?
What sons will ye bring forth — mean-souled like you,

Or, like your parents, brave — to blush like girls,
And say, 'Our fathers were afraid to die!'
Ye will not dare to raise heroic eyes
Unto the eyes of aliens. In the streets
Will women and young children point at you
Scornfully, and the sun will find you shamed,
And night refuse to shield you. What a life
Is this ye spin and fashion for yourselves!
And what new tortures of suspense and doubt
Will death invent for such as are afraid!
Acastus, thou my brother, in the field
Foremost, who greeted me with sanguine hands
From ruddy battle with a conqueror's face,
These honors wilt thou blot with infamy?
Nay, thou hast won no honors: a mere girl
Would do as much as thou at such a time,
In clamorous battle, 'midst tumultuous sounds,
Neighing of war-steeds, shouts of sharp command,
Snapping of shivered spears; for all are brave
When all men look to them expectantly;
But he is truly brave who faces death
Within his chamber, at a sudden call,
At night, when no man sees, content to die
When life can serve no longer those he loves.'
Then thus Acastus: 'Sister, I fear not
Death, nor the empty darkness of the grave,
And hold my life but as a little thing,
Subject unto my people's call, and Fate.
But if 't is little, no greater is the king's;
And though my heart bleeds sorely, I recall
Astydamia, who thus would mourn for me.
We are not cowards, we youth of Thessaly,
And Thessaly — yea, all Greece — knoweth it;
Nor will we brook the name from even you,
Albeit a queen, and uttering these wild words
Through your unwonted sorrow.' Then she knew
That he stood firm, and turning from him, cried
To the king's parents: 'Are ye deaf with grief,
Pheres, Clymene? Ye can save your son,
Yet rather stand and weep with barren tears.
O, shame! to think that such gray, reverend hairs
Should cover such unvenerable heads!
What would ye lose? a remnant of mere life,
A few slight raveled threads, and give him years
To fill with glory. Who, when he is gone,
Will call you gentlest names this side of heaven,
Father and mother? Knew ye not this man
Ere he was royal, a poor, helpless child,
Crownless and kingdomless? One birth alone
Sufficeth not, Clymene: once again
You must give life with travail and strong pain.

Has he not lived to outstrip your swift hopes?
What mother can refuse a second birth
To such a son? But ye denying him,
What after-offering may appease the gods?
What joy outweigh the grief of this one day?
What clamor drown the hours' myriad tongues,
Crying, 'Your son, your son? where is your son,
Unnatural mother, timid, foolish man?'
Then Pheres gravely: 'These are graceless words
From you our daughter. Life is always life,
And death comes soon enough to such as we.
We twain are old and weak, have served our time,
And made our sacrifices. Let the young
Arise now in their turn and save the king.'
'O gods! look on your creatures! do ye see?
And seeing, have ye patience? Smite them all,
Unsparing, with dishonorable death.
Vile slaves! a woman teaches you to die.
Intrepid, with exalted steadfast soul,
Scorn in my heart, and love unutterable,
I yield the Fates my life, and like a god
Command them to revere that sacred head.
Thus kiss I thrice the dear, blind, holy eyes,
And bid them see; and thrice I kiss this brow,
And thus unfasten I the pale, proud lips
With fruitful kissings, bringing love and life,
And without fear or any pang, I breathe
My soul in him.'
'Alcestis, I awake.
I hear, I hear — unspeak thy reckless words!
For, lo! thy life-blood tingles in my veins,
And streameth through my body like new wine.
Behold! thy spirit dedicate revives
My pulse, and through thy sacrifice I breathe.
Thy lips are bloodless: kiss me not again.
Ashen thy cheeks, faded thy flowerlike hands.
O woman! perfect in thy womanhood
And in thy wifehood, I adjure thee now
As mother, by the love thou bearest our child,
In this thy hour of passion and of love,
Of sacrifice and sorrow, to unsay
Thy words sublime!' 'I die that thou mayest live.'
'And deemest thou that I accept the boon,
Craven, like these my subjects? Lo, my queen,
Is life itself a lovely thing, bare life?
And empty breath a thing desirable?
Or is it rather happiness and love
That make it precious to its inmost core?
When these are lost, are there not swords in Greece,
And flame and poison, deadly waves and plagues?
No man has ever lacked these things and gone

Unsatisfied. It is not these the gods refuse
(Nay, never clutch my sleeve and raise thy lip),
Not these I seek; but I will stab myself,
Poison my life and burn my flesh, with words,
And save or follow thee. Lo! hearken now:
I bid the gods take back their loathsome gifts:
I spurn them, and I scorn them, and I hate.
Will they prove deaf to this as to my prayers?
With tongue reviling, blasphemous, I curse,
With mouth polluted from deliberate heart.
Dishonored be their names, scorned be their priests,
Ruined their altars, mocked their oracles!
It is Admetus, King of Thessaly,
Defaming thus: annihilate him, gods!
So that his queen, who worships you, may live.'
He paused as one expectant; but no bolt
From the insulted heavens answered him,
But awful silence followed. Then a hand,
A boyish hand, upon his shoulder fell,
And turning, he beheld his shepherd boy,
Not wrathful, but divinely pitiful,
Who spake in tender, thrilling tones: 'The gods
Cannot recall their gifts. Blaspheme them not:
Bow down and worship rather. Shall he curse
Who sees not, and who hears not, — neither knows
Nor understands? Nay, thou shalt bless and pray, —
Pray, for the pure heart, purged by prayer, divines
And seeth when the bolder eyes are blind.
Worship and wonder, — these befit a man
At every hour; and mayhap will the gods
Yet work a miracle for knees that bend
And hands that supplicate.'
Then all they knew
A sudden sense of awe, and bowed their heads
Beneath the stripling's gaze: Admetus fell,
Crushed by that gentle touch, and cried aloud:
'Pardon and pity! I am hard beset.'

There waited at the doorway of the king
One grim and ghastly, shadowy, horrible,
Bearing the likeness of a king himself,
Erect as one who serveth not, upon
His head a crown, within his fleshless hands
A sceptre, monstrous, winged, intolerable.
To him a stranger coming 'neath the trees,
Which slid down flakes of light, now on his hair,
Close-curled, now on his bared and brawny chest,
Now on his flexile, vine-like veinéd limbs,
With iron network of strong muscle thewed,
And godlike brows and proud mouth unrelaxed.
Firm was his step; no superfluity

Of indolent flesh impeded this man's strength.
Slender and supple every perfect limb,
Beautiful with the glory of a man.
No weapons bare he, neither shield: his hands
Folded upon his breast, his movements free
Of all incumbrance. When his mighty strides
Had brought him nigh the waiting one, he paused:
'Whose palace this? and who art thou, grim shade?'
'The palace of the King of Thessaly,
And my name is not strange unto thine ears;
For who hath told men that I wait for them,
The one sure thing on earth? Yet all they know,
Unasking and yet answered. I am Death,
The only secret that the gods reveal.
But who art thou who darest question me?'
'Alcides; and that thing I dare not do
Hath found no name. Whom here awaitest thou?'
'Alcestis, Queen of Thessaly, — a queen
Who wooed me as the bridegroom woos the bride,
For her life sacrificed will save her lord
Admetus, as the Fates decreed. I wait
Impatient, eager; and I enter soon,
With darkening wing, invisible, a god,
And kiss her lips, and kiss her throbbing heart,
And then the tenderest hands can do no more
Than close her eyes and wipe her cold, white brow,
Inurn her ashes and strew flowers above.'
'This woman is a god, a hero, Death.
In this her sacrifice I see a soul
Luminous, starry: earth can spare her not:
It is not rich enough in purity
To lose this paragon. Save her, O Death!
Thou surely art more gentle than the Fates,
Yet these have spared her lord, and never meant
That she should suffer, and that this their grace,
Beautiful, royal on one side, should turn
Sudden and show a fearful, fatal face.'
'Nay, have they not? O fond and foolish man,
Naught comes unlooked for, unforeseen by them.
Doubt when they favor thee, though thou mayest laugh
When they have scourged thee with an iron scourge.
Behold, their smile is deadlier than their sting,
And every boon of theirs is double-faced.
Yea, I am gentler unto ye than these:
I slay relentless, but when have I mocked
With poisoned gifts, and generous hands that smite
Under the flowers? for my name is Truth.
Were this fair queen more fair, more pure, more chaste,
I would not spare her for your wildest prayer
Nor her best virtue. Is the earth's mouth full?
Is the grave satisfied? Discrown me then,

For life is lord, and men may mock the gods
With immortality.' 'I sue no more,
But I command thee spare this woman's life,
Or wrestle with Alcides.' 'Wrestle with thee,
Thou puny boy!' And Death laughed loud, and swelled
To monstrous bulk, fierce-eyed, with outstretched wings,
And lightnings round his brow; but grave and firm,
Strong as a tower, Alcides waited him,
And these began to wrestle, and a cloud
Impenetrable fell, and all was dark.

'Farewell, Admetus and my little son,
Eumelus, O these clinging baby hands!
Thy loss is bitter, for no chance, no fame,
No wealth of love, can ever compensate
For a dead mother. Thou, O king, fulfill
The double duty: love him with my love,
And make him bold to wrestle, shiver spears,
Noble and manly, Grecian to the bone;
And tell him that his mother spake with gods.
Farewell, farewell! Mine eyes are growing blind:
The darkness gathers. O my heart, my heart!'
No sound made answer save the cries of grief
From all the mourners, and the suppliance
Of strick'n Admetus: ' O have mercy, gods!
O gods, have mercy, mercy upon us!'
Then from the dying woman's couch again
Her voice was heard, but with strange sudden tones:
'Lo, I awake, — the light comes back to me.
What miracle is this?' And thunders shook
The air, and clouds of mighty darkness fell,
And the earth trembled, and weird, horrid sounds
Were heard of rushing wings and fleeing feet,
And groans; and all were silent, dumb with awe,
Saving the king, who paused not in his prayer:
'Have mercy, gods!' and then again, 'O gods,
Have mercy!'

Through the open casement poured
Bright floods of sunny light; the air was soft,
Clear, delicate as though a summer storm
Had passed away; and those there standing saw,
Afar upon the plain, Death fleeing thence,
And at the doorway, weary, well-nigh spent,
Alcides, flushed with victory.

The Guardian Of The Red Disk

Spoken by a Citizen of Malta - 1300.

A curious title held in high repute,
One among many honors, thickly strewn
On my lord Bishop's head, his grace of Malta.
Nobly he bears them all,-with tact, skill, zeal,
Fulfills each special office, vast or slight,
Nor slurs the least minutia,-therewithal
Wears such a stately aspect of command,
Broad-checked, broad-chested, reverend, sanctified,
Haloed with white about the tonsure's rim,
With dropped lids o'er the piercing Spanish eyes
(Lynx-keen, I warrant, to spy out heresy);
Tall, massive form, o'ertowering all in presence,
Or ere they kneel to kiss the large white hand.
His looks sustain his deeds,-the perfect prelate,
Whose void chair shall be taken, but not filled.
You know not, who are foreign to the isle,
Haply, what this Red Disk may be, he guards.
'T is the bright blotch, big as the Royal seal,
Branded beneath the beard of every Jew.
These vermin so infest the isle, so slide
Into all byways, highways that may lead
Direct or roundabout to wealth or power,
Some plain, plump mark was needed, to protect
From the degrading contact Christian folk.

The evil had grown monstrous: certain Jews
Wore such a haughty air, had so refined,
With super-subtile arts, strict, monkish lives,
And studious habit, the coarse Hebrew type,
One might have elbowed in the public mart
Iscariot,-nor suspected one's soul-peril.
Christ's blood! it sets my flesh a-creep to think!
We may breathe freely now, not fearing taint,
Praise be our good Lord Bishop! He keeps count
Of every Jew, and prints on cheek or chin
The scarlet stamp of separateness, of shame.

No beard, blue-black, grizzled or Judas-colored,
May hide that damning little wafer-flame.
When one appears therewith, the urchins know
Good sport's at hand; they fling their stones and mud,
Sure of their game. But most the wisdom shows
Upon the unbelievers' selves; they learn
Their proper rank; crouch, cringe, and hide,-lay by
Their insolence of self-esteem; no more
Flaunt forth in rich attire, but in dull weeds,
Slovenly donned, would slink past unobserved;
Bow servile necks and crook obsequious knees,
Chin sunk in hollow chest, eyes fixed on earth
Or blinking sidewise, but to apprehend

Whether or not the hated spot be spied.
I warrant my Lord Bishop has full hands,
Guarding the Red Disk-lest one rogue escape!

How Long?

How long, and yet how long,
Our leaders will we hail from over seas,
Master and kings from feudal monarchies,
And mock their ancient song
With echoes weak of foreign melodies?

That distant isle mist-wreathed,
Mantled in unimaginable green,
Too long hath been our mistress and our queen.
Our fathers have bequeathed
Too deep a love for her, our hearts within.

She made the whole world ring
With the brave exploits of her children strong,
And with the matchless music of her song.
Too late, too late we cling
To alien legends, and their strains prolong.

This fresh young world I see,
With heroes, cities, legends of her own;
With a new race of men, and overblown
By winds from sea to sea,
Decked with the majesty of every zone.

I see the glittering tops
Of snow-peaked mounts, the wid'ning vale's expanse,
Large prairies where free herds of horses prance,
Exhaustless wealth of crops,
In vast, magnificent extravagance.

These grand, exuberant plains,
These stately rivers, each with many a mouth,
The exquisite beauty of the soft-aired south,
The boundless seas of grains,
Luxuriant forests' lush and splendid growth.

The distant siren-song
Of the green island in the eastern sea,
Is not the lay for this new chivalry.
It is not free and strong
To chant on prairies 'neath this brilliant sky.

The echo faints and fails;

It suiteth not, upon this western plain,
Out voice or spirit; we should stir again
The wilderness, and make the vales
Resound unto a yet unheard-of strain.

Heroes

In rich Virginian woods,
The scarlet creeper reddens over graves,
Among the solemn trees enlooped with vines;
Heroic spirits haunt the solitudes,-
The noble souls of half a million braves,
Amid the murmurous pines.

Ah! who is left behind,
Earnest and eloquent, sincere and strong,
To consecrate their memories with words
Not all unmeet? with fitting dirge and song
To chant a requiem purer than the wind,
And sweeter than the birds?

Here, though all seems at peace,
The placid, measureless sky serenely fair,
The laughter of the breeze among the leaves,
The bars of sunlight slanting through the trees,
The reckless wild-flowers blooming everywhere,
The grasses' delicate sheaves,-

Nathless each breeze that blows,
Each tree that trembles to its leafy head
With nervous life, revives within our mind,
Tender as flowers of May, the thoughts of those
Who lie beneath the living beauty, dead,-
Beneath the sunshine, blind.

For brave dead soldiers, these:
Blessings and tears of aching thankfulness,
Soft flowers for the graves in wreaths enwove,
The odorous lilac of dear memories,
The heroic blossoms of the wilderness,
And the rich rose of love.

But who has sung their praise,
Not less illustrious, who are living yet?
Armies of heroes, satisfied to pass
Calmly, serenely from the whole world's gaze,
And cheerfully accept, without regret,
Their old life as it was,

With all its petty pain,
Its irritating littleness and care;
They who have scaled the mountain, with content
Sublime, descend to live upon the plain;
Steadfast as though they breathed the mountain-air
Still, wheresoe'er they went.

They who were brave to act,
And rich enough their action to forget;
Who, having filled their day with chivalry,
Withdraw and keep their simpleness intact,
And all unconscious add more lustre yet
Unto their victory.

On the broad Western plains
Their patriarchal life they live anew;
Hunters as mighty as the men of old,
Or harvesting the plenteous, yellow grains,
Gathering ripe vintage of dusk bunches blue,
Or working mines of gold;

Or toiling in the town,
Armed against hindrance, weariness, defeat,
With dauntless purpose not to serve or yield,
And calm, defiant, they struggle on,
As sturdy and as valiant in the street,
As in the camp and field.

And those condemned to live,
Maimed, helpless, lingering still through suffering years,
May they not envy now the restful sleep
Of the dear fellow-martyrs they survive?
Not o'er the dead, but over these, your tears,
O brothers, ye may weep!

New England fields I see,
The lovely, cultured landscape, waving grain,
Wide haughty rivers, and pale, English skies.
And lo! a farmer ploughing busily,
Who lifts a swart face, looks upon the plain,-
I see, in his frank eyes,

The hero's soul appear.
Thus in the common fields and streets they stand;
The light that on the past and distant gleams,
They cast upon the present and the near,
With antique virtues from some mystic land,
Of knightly deeds and dreams.

Arabesque

On a background of pale gold
I would trace with quaint design,
Penciled fine,
Brilliant-colored, Moorish scenes,
Mosques and crescents, pages, queens,
Line on line,
That the prose-world of to-day
Might the gorgeous Past's array
Once behold.

On the magic painted shield
Rich Granada's Vega green
Should be seen;
Crystal fountains, coolness flinging,
Hanging gardens' skyward springing
Emerald sheen;
Ruddy when the daylight falls,
Crowned Alhambra's beetling walls
Stand revealed;

Balconies that overbrow
Field and city, vale and stream.
In a dream
Lulled the drowsy landscape basks;
Mark the gleam
Silvery of each white-swathed peak!
Mountain-airs caress the cheek,
Fresh from the snow.

Here in Lindaraxa's bower
The immortal roses bloom;
In the room
Lion-guarded, marble-paven,
Still the fountain leaps to heaven.
But the doom
Of the banned and stricken race
Overshadows every place,
Every hour.

Where fair Lindaraxa dwelt
Flits the bat on velvet wings;
Mute the strings
Of the broken mandoline;
The Pavilion of the Queen
Widely flings
Vacant windows to the night;
Moonbeams kiss the floor with light
Where she knelt.

Through these halls that people stepped
Who through darkling centuries
Held the keys
Of all wisdom, truth, and art,
In a Paradise apart,
Lapped in ease,
Sagely pondering deathless themes,
While, befooled with monkish dreams,
Europe slept.

Where shall they be found today?
Yonder hill that frets the sky
'The last Sigh
Of the Moor' is named still.
There the ill-starred Boabdil
Bade good-by
To Granada and to Spain,
Where the Crescent ne'er again
Holdeth sway.

Vanished like the wind that blows,
Whither shall we seek their trace
On earth's face?
The gigantic wheel of fate,
Crushing all things soon or late,
Now a race,
Now a single life o'erruns,
Now a universe of suns,
Now a rose.

Don Pedrillo

Not a lad in Saragossa
Nobler-featured, haughtier-tempered,
Than the Alcalde's youthful grandson,
Donna Clara's boy Pedrillo.

Handsome as the Prince of Evil,
And devout as St. Ignatius.
Deft at fence, unmatched with zither,
Miniature of knightly virtues.

Truly an unfailing blessing
To his pious, widowed mother,
To the beautiful, lone matron
Who forswore the world to rear him.

For her beauty hath but ripened
In such wise as the pomegranate

Putteth by her crown of blossoms,
For her richer crown of fruitage.

Still her hand is claimed and courted,
Still she spurns her proudest suitors,
Doting on a phantom passion,
And upon her boy Pedrillo.

Like a saint lives Donna Clara,
First at matins, last at vespers,
Half her fortune she expendeth
Buying masses for the needy.

Visiting the poor afflicted,
Infinite is her compassion,
Scorning not the Moorish beggar,
Nor the wretched Jew despising.

And-a scandal to the faithful,
E'en she hath been known to welcome
To her castle the young Rabbi,
Offering to his tribe her bounty.

Rarely hath he crossed the threshold,
Yet the thought that he hath crossed it,
Burns like poison in the marrow
Of the zealous youth Pedrillo.

By the blessed Saint Iago,
He hath vowed immortal hatred
To these circumcised intruders
Who pollute the soil of Spaniards.

Seated in his mother's garden,
At high noon the boy Pedrillo
Playeth with his favorite parrot,
Golden-green with streaks of scarlet.

'Pretty Dodo, speak thy lesson,'
Coaxed Pedrillo-'thief and traitor'-
'Thief and traitor'-croaked the parrot,
'Is the yellow-skirted Rabbi.'

And the boy with peals of laughter,
Stroked his favorite's head of emerald,
Raised his eyes, and lo! before him
Stood the yellow-skirted Rabbi.

In his dark eyes gleamed no anger,
No hot flush o'erspread his features.
'Neath his beard his pale lips quivered,

And a shadow crossed his forehead.

Very gentle was his aspect,
And his voice was mild and friendly,
'Evil words, my son, thou speakest,
Teaching to the fowls of heaven.

'In our Talmud it stands written,
Thrice curst is the tongue of slander,
Poisoning also with its victim,
Him who speaks and him who listens.'

But no whit abashed, Pedrillo,
'What care I for curse of Talmud?
'T is no slander to speak evil
Of the murderers of our Saviour.

'To your beard I will repeat it,
That I only bide my manhood,
To wreak all my lawful hatred,
On thyself and on thy people.'

Very gently spoke the Rabbi,
'Have a care, my son Pedrillo,
Thou art orphaned, and who knoweth
But thy father loved this people?'

'Think you words like these will touch me?
Such I laugh to scorn, sir Rabbi,
From high heaven, my sainted father
On my deeds will smile in blessing.

'Loyal knight was he and noble,
And my mother oft assures me,
Ne'er she saw so pure a Christian,
'T is from him my zeal deriveth.'

'What if he were such another
As myself who stand before thee?'
'I should curse the hour that bore me,
I should die of shame and horror.'

'Harsher is thy creed than ours;
For had I a son as comely
As Pedrillo, I would love him,
Love him were he thrice a Christian.

'In his youth my youth renewing
Pamper, fondle, die to serve him,
Only breathing through his spirit-
Couldst thou not love such a father?'

Faltering spoke the deep-voiced Rabbi,
With white lips and twitching fingers,
Then in clear, young, steady treble,
Answered him the boy Pedrillo:

'At the thought my heart revolteth,
All your tribe offend my senses,
They're an eyesore to my vision,
And a stench unto my nostrils.

'When I meet these unbelievers,
With thick lips and eagle noses,
Thus I scorn them, thus revile them,
Thus I spit upon their garment.'

And the haughty youth passed onward,
Bearing on his wrist his parrot,
And the yellow-skirted Rabbi
With bowed head sought Donna Clara.

The Garden Of Adonis

(The Garden of Life in Spenser's 'Faerie Queene.')

It is no fabled garden in the skies,
But bloometh here— this is no world of death;
And nothing that once liveth, ever dies,
And naught that breathes can ever cease to breathe,
And naught that bloometh ever withereth.
The gods can ne'er take back their gifts from men,
They gave us life,— they cannot take again.

Who hath known Death, and who hath seen his face?
On what high mountain have ye met with him?
Within what lowest valley is there trace
Of his feared footsteps? in what forest dim,
In what great city, in what lonely ways?
Nay, there is no such god, but one called Change,
And all he does is beautiful and strange.

It is but Change that lays our darlings low,
And, though we doubt and fear, forsakes them not.
Where red lips smiled do sweetest roses blow,
And star-flowers bloom above the lovely spot
Where gleamed the eyes, with blue forget-me-not.
And through the grasses runs the same wave there
We knew of old within the golden hair.

Dig in the earth— ye shall not surely find
Death or death's semblance; only roots of flowers,
And all fair, goodly things there live enshrined,
With the foundations of the glad green bowers,
Through which the sunshine comes in golden showers.
And all the blossoms that this earth enwreathe,
Are for assurance that there is no death.

O mother, raise thy tear-bathed lids again:
Thy child died not, he only liveth more
His soul is in the sunshine and the rain,
His life is in the waters and the shore,
He is around thee all the wide world o'er;
The daisy thou hast plucked smiles back at thee,
Because it doth again its mother see.

What noble deed that ever lived, is dead,
Or yet hath lost its power to inspire
Courage in hearts that sicken, and to shed
New faith and hope when hands and footsteps tire,
And make sad, downcast eyes look upward higher?
Yea, all men see and know it, whence it came;
It purifies them like a burning flame.

And dreams? What dreams were ever lost and gone,
But wandering in strange lands we found again?
When least we think of these dear birdlings flown,
We find that bright and fresh they still remain.
The garden of all life is round us then;
And he is blind who doth not know and see,
And praise the gods for immortality.

Orpheus

ORPHEUS.
Laughter and dance, and sounds of harp and lyre,
Piping of flutes, singing of festal songs,
Ribbons of flame from flaunting torches, dulled
By the broad summer sunshine, these had filled
Since the high noon the pillared vestibules,
The peristyles and porches, in the house
Of the bride's father. Maidens, garlanded
With rose and myrtle dedicate to Love,
Adorned with chaplets fresh the bride, and veiled
The shining head and wistful, girlish face,
Ineffable sweetness of divided lips,
Large light of clear, gray eyes, low, lucid brows,
White as a cloud, beneath pale, clustering gold.
When sunless skies uncertain twilight cast,

That makes a friend's face as an alien's strange,
Investing with a foreign mystery
The dear green fields about our very home.
Then waiting stood the gilded chariot
Before the porch, and from the vine-wreathed door,
Issued the white-veiled bride, while jocund youths
And mænads followed her with dance and song.
She came with double glory; for her lord,
Son of Apollo and Calliope,
Towered beside her, beautiful in limb
And feature, as though formed to magic strains,
Like the Bœotian city, that arose
In airy structures to Amphion's lute.
The light serene shone from his brow and eyes,
Of one whose lofty thoughts keep consonance
With the celestial music of the spheres.
His smile was fluent, and his speech outsang
The cadences of soft-stringed instruments.
He to the chariot led Eurydice,
And these twain, mounting with their paranymph,
Drove onward through the dusky twilit fields,
Preceded by the nymphs and singing youths,
And boys diffusing light and odors warm,
With flaming brands of aromatic woods,
And matrons bearing symbols of the life
Of careful wives, the distaff and the sieve;
And followed by the echoes of their songs,
The fragrance crushed from moist and trodden grass,
The blessing of the ever-present gods,
Whom they invoked with earnest hymns and prayer.
From Orpheus' portico, festooned with vines,
Issued a flood of rare, ambrosial light,
As though Olympian portals stood ajar,
And Hymen, radiant by his torch's flame,
Mystic with saffron vest and purple, stood
With hands munificent to greet and bless.
Ripe fruits were poured upon the married pair
Alighting, and the chariot wheels were burnt,
A token that the bride returned no more
Unto her father's house. With step resolved,
She crossed the threshold soft with flowers, secure
That his heroic soul who guided her,
Was potent and alert to grace her life,
With noble outlines and ideal hues,
Uplifting it to equal height with his.

EPITHALAMIUM. TO ZEUS.

Because thou art enthroned beyond our reach,
Behind the brightest and the farthest star,
And silence is as eloquent as speech,
To thee who knowest us for what we are,

We bring thee naught save brief and simple prayer,
Strong in its naked, frank sincerity.
Send sacred joys of marriage to this pair,
With fertile increase and prosperity.
Three nymphs had met beneath an oak that cast
Cool, dappled shadow on the glowing grass,
And liquid gleam of the translucent brook.
The air was musical with frolic sounds
Of feminine voices, and of laughter blithe.
Patines of sunshine fell like mottled gold
On the rose-white of bright bare limbs and neck,
On flowing, snowy mantles, and again
With sudden splendor on the gloriole
Of warm, rich hair. The fairest nymph reclined
Beneath the tree, and leaned her yellow head,
With its crisp, clustering rings, against the trunk,
And dipped her pure feet in the colorless brook,
Stirring the ripples into circles wide,
With cool, delicious plashings in the stream.
Her young companions lay upon the grass,
With indolent eyes half closed, and parted lips
Half-smiling, in the languor of the noon.
But suddenly these twain, arising, cried,
Startled and sharply, 'Lo, Eurydice,
Behold!' and she, uplifting frightened eyes,
Saw a strange shepherd watching with bold glance.
Veiling their faces with their mantles light,
Her sisters fled swift-footed, with shrill cries,
Adown the meadow, but her wet feet clung
To the dry grasses and the earthy soil.
'Eurydice, I love thee! fear me not,
For I am Aristæus, with gray groves
Of hoary olives, and innumerous flocks,
And precious swarms of yellow-vested bees.'
But she with sudden strength eluding him,
Sprang o'er the flowery turf, with back-blown hair,
And wing-like garments, shortened breath, and face
Kindled with shame and terror. In her flight
She ran through fatal flowers and tangled weeds,
And thick rank grass beside a stagnant pool,
When, with a keen and breathless cry of pain,
Abrupt she fell amidst the tall, green reeds.
Then Aristæus reached her, as a snake
Crept back in sinuous lines amidst the slime.
Desire was changed to pity, when he saw
The wounded dryad in her agony
Strive vainly to escape, repelling him
With feeble arms. 'Forgive me, nymph,' he cried;
'I will not touch, save with most reverent hands,
Thy sacred form. But let me bear thee hence,
And soothe thy bruise with healing herbs. 'Too late,

Leave me,' she sighed, 'and lead thou Orpheus here,
That I may see him ere the daylight fails.'
He left her pale with suffering, earth seemed strange
Unto her eyes, who knew she looked her last
On level-stretching meadows, hazy hills,
And all the light and color of the sky.
Brief as a dream she saw her happy life,
Her father's face, her mother's blessed eyes,
The hero who, unheralded, appeared,
And all was changed, all things put forth a voice,
As in the season of the singing birds.
She looked around revived, and saw again
The lapsing river and abiding sky.
Across the sunny fields came Aristæus,
With Orpheus following, and after these,
Sad nymphs and heroes grave with sympathy.
Quite calm she lay, and almost wished to die
Before they reached her, if the throbbing pain
Of limb and heart could only thus be stilled.
But Orpheus hastened to her side, and mourned,
'Eurydice, Eurydice! Remain,
For there is no delight of speech nor song
Among the dead. Will the gods jest with me,
And call this life, which must forevermore
Be but a void, a hunger, a desire,
A stretching out of empty hands to grasp
What earth nor sea nor heaven will restore?
Is this the life that I conceived and sang,
Rich with all noble opportunities
And beautiful realities?' But she:
'Brave Orpheus, search thou not the eternal gods,
Surely they love us dearer than we know.
Do thou refrain, for yet I hold my faith.
When I am gone, thou still wilt have thy lyre;
Love it and cherish, it is Fate's best gift,
And with death's clearer vision, I can see
That in all ages men will be upraised
Nearer to gods through this than through aught else.
My death may but inspire a larger note,
A passionate cadence to thy strain, which else
Were not quite human, and thus incomplete.
And with this thought I am content to die.
Cease not to sing to me when I am gone;
Thy voice will reach me in the farthest spheres,
Or wake me out of silence. Now begin,
That I may float on those celestial waves
Into the darkness, as I oft have longed.'

ORPHEUS.
Once in a wild, bright vision, came to me
Beautiful music, luminous as morn,

An effluence of light and rapture born,
With eyes as full of splendor as the sea;
Dazzling as youth, with pinions frail as air,
Yet potent to uplift and soar as prayer.
Again I see her, cypress in her wreath,
Sad with all grave and tender mysteries;
Tears in her unimaginable eyes,
That look their first with wondering awe on Death.
Never again, in all the after years,
Will her lips laugh with utter mirthfulness;
Nor the strange longing in her eyes grow less,
Nor any time dispel their mist of tears.
Yea, with new numbers she completes her strain,
A song unsung before by gods or men;
But she hath lost, ah! lost for evermore,
The ringing note of joy ineffable,
The high assurance proud, that all is well,
The glad refrain that pealed from shore to shore.
O lyre, thou hast done with joyous things,
Triumphant ecstasies, exultant song;
Of subtle pain, keen anguish, hopeless wrong,
I fashion now another of thy strings,
And strike thee with a strong hand passionate,
Into a fuller music, adequate
Unto a soul that seeks insatiably,
With fond, illusive hope and faith divine;
For through all ages will my soul seek thine,
Eurydice, my lost Eurydice!
What solace to lament with empty hands
And smitten heart, above a mound of earth,
Vivid with mockery of perpetual flowers,
O'er one small urn that holds beneath its lid,
With over measure, all the flameless dust
And soulless ashes of our love? Yet this
Was Orpheus' life, to mourn beside the grave,
From his stringed lyre compelling wild response
And thrilling intonation of his grief,
That made the hearts of gnarled and knotty oaks
Ache as with human sympathy, and rived
The adamantine centre of the rock,
And lured the forest beasts, and hushed the birds,
Mavis and lark, while with wide, awful wings,
The eagle shadowed his exalted brow.
'Surely,' he cried, 'the senseless dust hears not,
More than the burnt brand hears old natural sounds
Innumerable rustle of young leaves.
It cannot be that only these remain,
The ashes of her glittering limbs, warm flesh,
And blessed hair, my love had more than these
Where is the vital soul, that was to me
An inspiration and an influence?

The gods are not unstable like rash man,
Aimlessly to create and discreate,
With cruel and capricious fantasy,
For thus the immaculate skies would be a lie;
Eurydice is but withdrawn from me,
And disembodied, while mine eyesight blinds,
My senses are a hindrance, and obstruct
The accurate perception of my soul.
When mine own spirit, nightly disenthralled,
Soars to the land of dreams, whose boundaries,
By day, loom infinitely far and vague,
And yet, at night, become our very home,
There still I see thee with the same bright form,
The same auroral eyes that made for me
Perpetual morning; and I stretch mine arms
Hungering after thee, and, calling, wake
Unto the vapid glare of languid dawn.
Yet all these things address my very soul,
Telling it that thou art not dead; for death
Is but the incarnation of man's fears;
Gods do not recognize it. If thou art
(As I have faith) in the known universe,
Yea, though it be in the extremest land,
Beyond the sunset, with its shining isles,
I will go forth and seek thee, nor will cease
To mourn thee and desire, till I have found.'
Thus Orpheus fared across the full-fed streams
Of Hebrus and of Strymon, and beyond
The purple outlines and aerial crags,
Snow-glittering of Scardus, Rhodope,
And grand Orbelus; through fair, fertile fields
Of Thessaly with increase of ripe corn,
Through Attica, Bœotia and Eubœa,
And southward to the royal-citied state,
Beautiful Corinth, throned upon the base
Of green Acrocorinthus, whose soft slope
Was dedicate with temples to the gods,
And towering over all the sacred shrine
Of Aphrodite. Upward from the town
The mountain rose defensive, where the walls
Of Corinth ended, and beyond the gates,
The radiant plain of the Corinthian Gulf
Stretched infinitely. Orpheus rested here,
Till he bethought him to ascend the mount,
With offerings at Aphrodite's shrine
Not sanguine victims, but fresh myrtle wreath
And faultless rose—to sue the oracle
For help and guidance.
All the town was still,
The bright red band of sunrise lit the sky
Above the dark blue gulf, and Orpheus heard

A hundred birds saluting, from the brake,
Aurora, and cool rush of waterfalls.
Made murmurous music, while Athené breathed
The vigor of the morning in his soul.
Up the steep mountain side he passed, beyond
The silver growth of olives, and the belt
Of pines, to where the foam-white temple stood,
Smitten at once by all the beams of morn.
He saw the double peak, rose-white with snow
And early sunshine, of Parnassus cleave
The northern sky, and sacred Helicon
Erect its head, crowned with the Muses' grove,
The Bay of Crissa and Corinthian Gulf,
Below flashed restless, and a path of gold
Divided with clear, tremulous light the waves.
From the large beauty of the morn, he went
Into the holy limits of the shrine,
With warm air heavy with the odorous rose.

ORPHEUS.

I put into my prayer to thee, O mother,
The tumult and the passion of the ocean,
The unflecked purity of winnowed foam-wreaths;
To thee who sprang from these, the incarnation
Of all the huge sea holds of grace or splendor,
With its own light between thine amorous eyelids.
For I, in thy most sacred cause a pilgrim,
Have wandered tireless, from Thrace to Corinth,
'Midst foreign scenes and alien men and women.
And at my right hand Grief incessant follows,
And at my left walks Memory with the semblance
Of lost Eurydice's ethereal beauty.
Infatuate I gaze, until the vision
Thrills me to madness, and I start and tremble,
Remembering also Grief is my companion.
Onward through spacious fields, by copious waters,
Through purple growth of amaranth and crocus,
And past the marble beauty of great cities,
We three have journeyed, strangers saw me reckless,
And knew at once that I had walked with sorrow,
And that the gods had chosen me their victim.
Are all my carols useless, worse than useless?
Shall my long pilgrimage, thus unrewarded,
End at the blank, insuperable ocean?
Hast thou no wise compassion, goddess, mother?
In all the measureless years' unfathomed chances,
Is the dear past to be repeated never?
O supreme mother! crowned with blessed poppy
As well as myrtle, bring her here, or compass
My soul with death, that elsewhere I may seek her.
He ceased, and through the temple spread a mist

Ambrosial, and above the shrine a star
Serenely brightened, and a heavenly voice
Made sweet response: ' Love guides himself thy course
To the last sea-girt rock. No worthy soul
May ever truly seek, and fail to find.'
Still southward Orpheus journeyed, till he reached
Cape Tænarus, the last bleak point of Greece,
Desolate o'er an infinite waste of waves,
While sunset lit the western sea and sky
With yellow floods of warm, diffusive light,
Kindling his serious face and earnest eyes,
And glittering on his lyre. Long time he stood,
And gazed upon the trouble of the waves,
Expectant of a word, a sign and still
No answer made the wild, indifferent sea.
Impetuous, he smote his quivering lyre
To reckless and sonorous melody,
Vibrating o'er the watery turbulence.
Then far below its western bath, the sun
Dipped and was gone, and all the sea was gray.
Still through the air rang those imploring notes,
Unutterably plaintive— till there came
From out the ocean cave of Tænarus
The shining forms of Oceanides,
With myriad faces raised supremely fair,
And myriad arms that beckoned as he sang.
Behold! a stir amidst the frothing brine,
As though upheaved by powers submarine,
In implicate confusion, wave on wave,
Then rose with windy manes and fiery eyes,
Proudly careering, the immortal steeds,
Bearing, within the shell-shaped car, the god
Of august aspect and imperial port,
With such profusion of ambrosial locks
As curl around the very front of Zeus.
He with benign regard the minstrel viewed,
Then whirling thrice his massy trident, struck
The scarpéd promontory with its fork.
And Orpheus felt the solid basis yield,
And heard the hollow rumbling, as when earth
Rocks to her centre, and high hills spit flame.
And lo! he stood before a sulphurous throne,
Set in an open space, wherefrom there streamed
Four rivers stagnant, black. Here Ades reigned,
His very presence unto mortal sense
Oppressive as low thunder in the air.
The triple-headed guardian of his realm
Crouched at his feet, and in the dismal murk,
The hideous Harpies hovered o'er his head.
The serpent-haired Eumenides stood near,
Brow-bound with sanguine fillets, and the Fates

Wielded the distaff, spindle, and sharp shears.
The air was dense with noisome influence,
And shadowy apparitions seemed to float
Athwart the dusk. But on the infernal throne
Conspicuous in beauty, by her lord,
Persephone was seated. Wonderment
Looked from her eyes, in seeing him, no god,
Who came before his time among the dead,
Unarmed with spear or shield, a glistening lyre
Nigh slipping from the loose grasp of his hands.
'Who comes unsummoned to my realm?' began
The baleful godhead in discordant tones,
Widely reverberant; and the low, clear voice
Of Orpheus answered: 'One who would remain,
If but the impotent body could be free
To follow the desires of the soul,
Orpheus, an unskilled singer.' 'Birth and death
Are preordained for thee, presumptuous man.
What narrow space of time the Fates accord,
'Twould best become thee to bear worthily,
With dignity, and leave the rest to them,
The end as the beginning.' 'Plead for me,
O beautiful Persephone, behold!
Eurydice was snatched with violent hand
From out mine eager arms, and I have sought
Her image o'er the peopled earth in vain.'
Then she: 'I may not summon her, nor hope
To swerve the haughty purpose of my lord.
With influence of thy familiar voice,
If thou canst touch her spirit, she is thine.'
But Ades: 'Who recalls the dead by prayer?
They whose calm souls are once possessed by death,
Find such a solid joy in grasping firm,
After life's phantasms, this reality,
That wisdom, grief, nor love persuadeth them
Their liberated spirits to confine
With fleshly limitations. Nathless sing,
And prove life's glittering evanescence vain,
Outweighed by death's sublime security.'

ORPHEUS.
I render thanks, eternal gods, that ye
Empower myself to call Eurydice.
Man only can fulfill his own desire;
And if I fail, the sorrow rests with me.
Ye give what we deserve; I pray alone
Ne'er to be cursed with what I have not won.
And to whom else would I intrust my lyre,
This supreme invocation to intone?
But in myself I feel the love, the power,
The lyric inspiration, while the flower

Of all my life brings forth its proper fruit,
In this my loftiest, most godlike hour.
If I could make ye feel the agony
Of the strong man, O gods, condemned to see
The light fail from dear eyes, the white lips mute,
The elusive soul take flight eternally
To where we cannot follow it nor find,
With the most subtle searchings of the mind,
With the most passionate longings of the soul,
Deaf, unresponsive as the empty wind;
Then would your pity as your power be,
'Twould crown us all with immortality,
And grace us with completeness, make us whole,
Worthy to be the peers of deity.
For we are mighty now to slay and bless,
Yea, gifted with strange strength of steadfastness,
To conquer bodiless and viewless foes
Within ourselves, yet in our helplessness,
As children, in the presence of this Death,
Whom nor revolt nor patience conquereth,
Implacable, with grim mouth fastened close,
That with no hope our anguish answereth.
Resound with wildest utterance, O my lyre;
Let each note be a living flame of fire,
To reach her, to burn through her, to compel,
Strong with the infinite strength of my desire.
I am no god, yet Fate, Eurydice,
A goddess for my slave hath given me,
Immortal Music, pure, ineffable;
And I send her, my handmaid, after thee.
If all wherein I put my faith as sure,
Be not delusions vain which death will cure;
If the sublime reliance of the soul
On her own powers be no empty lure,
Whereat the high gods laugh in bitter scorn;
If what I have achieved and what forborne,
Will lead me nearer to a worthy goal,
If all life's promises be not forsworn,
Eurydice, appear! Before mine eyes,
O gods, I see a formless essence rise,
That moulds itself unto the music's beat,
Appareled in the glory of the skies.
Now, while I ring a more celestial tone,
The spirit more divinely bright hath grown,
To larger modulations, strains complete,
The white limbs from the shapeless mist are won,
As from the bosom of a summer cloud,
Wherewith a goddess would her semblance shroud.
Is this mine own creation? Is it truth,
That with warm life I have blank air endowed?
The soft cloud parts asunder, yea, 'tis she!

Once more the face that was my star I see,
Crowned with the beauty of immortal youth,
Eurydice, my lost Eurydice!
Silent beside his silent, fallen lyre,
The singer stood, and clasped her in his arms,
Gazing upon this pale, fair face as one
Whose heart's supreme desire is satisfied.
'Is not this hour the hour I have foreseen,
Through all obstructions and infirmities
Of my mortality, and is it not
More glorious in fruition than I dreamed!
Yea, I have dreamed it all, eternal gods,
Even as now have pressed her to my heart
With the same clinging effort to retain,
And seen this breathing form, these lucent eyes
Vivid as now, instinct with life and love.
Yet have I waked to chill discouragement,
To vacant disappointment, and the sense
Of aching, unassuaged desire. O speak,
For in my dreams I never hear thy voice,
Save veiled and indistinct, a mockery
Of the old limpid music. Speak to me:
Thy flesh is warm, thy heart beats close to mine,
Thine upturned face is wet with human tears;
O speak to me, lest I should wake again
To barren fields and empty skies of Thrace.'
Then in low, natural tones, Eurydice:
'Thy voice hath reached me in the farthest spheres,
And waked me out of silence.' 'Follow me,
It is thyself, if I must wake from this,
'Twill be to death or madness. Follow me,
From darkness palpable, to earth, to light
Of ample skies, and freshness of blown grass
And rolling waters.' 'Hold!' the jarring voice
Of Ades interposed: ''Tis excellent
The attribute we gave thee, to convert
To such a weapon as may overcome
The old hereditary foes of man,
Sleep, death, corruption, and necessity.
But to reveal thyself the peer of gods,
Not only through inspired ecstasy,
But through a continent persistency,
This never was accomplished by thy race,
And thou must yet be tried. This soul is thine,
For thou hast won her from the jaws of Hell;
Yea, she may follow thee as free as light,
Lead thou the way and charm the hostile fiends.
Look forward ever; if thine eyes revert
But once to gaze on her, to reassure
Unworthy fears, or sate a mean desire,
Thou art not mate for us. She will dissolve

To empty air —never to be recalled.

ORPHEUS.
Back to the vital earth, O follow me,
Regained Eurydice.
To rippling well-heads and to sunlit plains,
Greened by soft wash of rains.
See orchards rosy with prolific bloom,
And vineyards' purple gloom.
Lulled by the languid flow of lilied streams,
There will I sing my dreams.
Behold! I chant a hymn of adoration,
Triumphant exultation,
For I can see, in all the universe,
No error and no curse.
The gods have naught withheld, in power and sway,
From him who will obey
Their own divine and everlasting laws.
Above the world's applause,
As vigorous as morning, he can rise,
Wrest the desired prize
From the clenched hands of Nemesis and Fate.
With victory elate,
I chant unmitigated prayer and praise
To gods who part our ways,
Seeing 'midst clamorous change incredible,
That all is ordered well.
In more harmonious strains, O lyre, express
My twice-born happiness;
Yea, utter and translate with larger sense
My rich experience,
That makes complete life's solemn threnody
Joy unalloyed and free,
Grief unexampled, victory at last,
When strife is overpast.
Through pathways hedged with horrors still they fared
Invulnerable. Darkness stayed them not,
Nor yet more dreadful light, revealing oft
The hideous fiends who rose on every side,
Huge shapes of ill, to gaze upon the twain.
A Greek, who, fleeing, smote a vibrant lyre,
That chimed to carols more divinely quired
Than those that fill with ravishment a grove,
Misty with moonlight, where the plain brown bird
Makes midnight vocal. Closely following him,
A woman with grave aspect, parted lips,
Upraising, in enthrallèd ecstasy,
Large eyes serene, fulfilled with holier light
For having pierced beyond the boundaries
Of time and of mortality. The day
Shone through the murk at last, and filled their path

With dusky sunbeams; and far-stretching fields
Of soft, delicious green, and crystal skies,
Encouraged them; all perils past save one.
But a black, stagnant river crawled along,
Spanned by no bridge, and ferried by no sail,
With muddy tide between the day and them.
And Orpheus with enamored eyes passed on,
And saw not how the loathsome waters crept,
Nor how his magic song enchanted them
To solid substance; but he missed at once
The footsteps light that had inspired his lay.
Impetuous he turned to reassure
His fearful soul, and sate his hungry eyes;
But as he turned, the inspiration fled,
His lips refused to frame the fruitless words,
His eyes beheld, O gods! Eurydice
Removed already far away from him,
By all the wide-expanded space, between
Our loftiest dream and our unworthy deed.
She gazed with no reproachful glance nor tears,
And Orpheus felt himself beneath her, fall,
Momently down from empyreal heights,
And lo! he stood within the fields of Thrace,
On earth familiar, 'neath familiar skies,
And heard a voice float through the shining air,
From unimaginable distances,
Faint as a dream, 'Farewell, farewell, farewell.'
'Woe! woe! what lamentations may express
The fullness of my new calamity!
I, overbearing, who presumed to reach
The lordly and severe stability
Of the immortals, whom may I invoke?
To whom may man appeal when he hath failed
Unto himself? What god will interpose
To thwart invincible necessity?
Lost, lost forever! I stood elevate,
For one brief moment dreaming I had won
The skill and power of true divinity.
Gods! with what lofty and superb disdain
Ye must look down on mine unworthy haste,
Ye, who with grandeur of sublime repose,
And majesty of patience, still abide
Invariable through eternity!
Alas! my mighty visions were to me
Auspicious omens, and they fed my heart
With vigor and encouragement; but now,
This was no dream; for Hope, full-flushed and fair,
Born, like the freshness of auroral dew,
From unseen air, and traceless vanishing,
Consorts not with this mighty goddess, Truth,
With solemn and unfathomable eyes,

For Truth is one with Death and Destiny.
With what a depth of meaning didst thou turn,
For the last time, to me, Eurydice,
A glory 'midst the darkness, with that glance
Of infinite compassion, hands outstretched,
As if to save the from mine own defect.
With what humiliation and despair
I saw thee rising unattainably!
The vault, the stream accursed had disappeared;
I was in Thrace uplooking to the sky.
O, to what harmonies I might have wed
The blessed tidings which all men await!
Now I can only make my song express
A distant echo, a suggestion vague,
Of the serene contentment of thy voice.
Sing this, my lyre, that all who hark to thee
With an attentive and a gentle ear,
May hear the promise, faint and yet assured,
Recall the grace and the deliciousness
Of immortality, and strive anew
Towards the ideal unattained by me,
Yet still accessible to stronger souls.'
Thus Orpheus, when the first wild burst of woe
Had passed; no need to seek her now;
No need to wander o'er the peopled earth.
Was he in truth a victim of the gods,
Or rather with a fairer fortune blest
Than happier men, selected for a fate
Divinely tragical, that he might know
The fullness of a life's experience,
And find expression adequate for all,
Simple as wisdom, and as dignified
As silence? From his kind he lived apart,
As one who cherishes a grief, nor seeks
Forgetfulness nor comfort; elevate
To glittering eminence by destiny,
And lonely through the privacy of woe
Beyond the reaches of man's sympathy.
Where lucid Hebrus bathes its golden sands,
He sat discoursing gracious harmonies,
Amidst the morning fields, when on his ears
Sounded with horrid dissonance the clang
Of smitten cymbals and the throb of drums.
But still the revelers remained unseen,
Till, rounding suddenly a neighboring hill,
The whole mad troop came dancing into sight.
First marched a jovial bacchanal, who bore
A crystal vessel, decked with branching vine,
Then youth and nymphs with ivy chapleted,
In purfled raiment of hues delicate,
With mitres, thyrsi, cymbals, drums and flutes,

Some balancing upon their graceful heads,
Regal with crisp-curled gold, their burdens light
Of baskets heaped with figs and dusky grapes.
And 'midst them all the sacrificial goat,
Adorned with berries. Thus the festal throng,
With wanton gestures, and with antic bounds,
And wild embracings, mad with wine, approached,
With peals of laughter, echoing faintly back
From jocund hill to hill, and lusty shouts
Of 'Bacché, Bacché!'

SONG.
With wassail all the night,
Celestial Bacchus, we have worshipped thee!
With riotous revel and with festal wine.
Still on the hills in early morning light,
With frolic dances and brisk jollity,
Our hymns of praise are thine.
For we have seen thee, god!
The fawn-skin slipping from thy shoulder bare,
Thy gestures lithe and loose, thine eyes that shine,
Thy rosy hands that waved a clustered rod
Of uncrushed grapes, and thine ambrosial hair,
Dripping with myrrh and wine.
Thou art not strict, severe,
Like loftier gods and ruthless goddesses,
Implacable like Pallas, Zeus, or Truth;
But to humanity akin and near,
Eager for folly, and the luxuries
Of lustful health and youth.
This crystal-vialed balm,
Divinely brewed, soothing as Lethe's streams,
Is the most generous gift of Deity,
Informing us with soft oblivion calm
Of Death and Fate, with joys beyond the dreams
Of grave sobriety.
Come, let us drink again.
Resound, O timbrels, and thou bird-voiced flute;
Thyrsus and pipes make shrill and dear acclaim,
To Bacchus, who impurples hill and plain
With vineyards bursting with increase of fruit,
Subtle as liquid flame.
Œoë! quaff and sing!
Who drinks no more, offends the deity
Of Bacchus! lo on Hebrus' grassy brink,
A minstrel sits, with gold lute glistening,
Marring our rites with stern solemnity,
Who doth not chant nor drink.
Ho! Orpheus, laugh again,
From mirthful heart, and join our happy throng;
Cease to lament with unappeased desire.

We bring a cordial for all grief and pain.
Add to the choral strain thy siren song,
And thine enchanted lyre.
For Fate hath answered thee
With cold derision; Death respondeth not.
Here is a god who soothes tire soul and sense
With sweet nepenthe,—thy Eurydice
Thou wilt not lure to earthly grove nor grot
With suasive eloquence.
Here, nymphs no whit less fair
Are waiting thee, with warm, caressing arms
And loving eyes, lips fit for gods to kiss,
And rosy shoulders, dimpling white and bare,
Pliant and graceful, with innumerous Charms,
To sate thy heart with bliss.

ORPHEUS.
Hence, thou ignoble throng!
Dare ye profane the splendid purity,
The high nobility of morn, with rites
Lewd and disgusting, and delirious song,
Completing in dear sunshine, shamelessly,
Rude orgies of wild nights?

BACCHANTES.
Ha! he insults the god,
With his presumptuous and impious scorn.
Avenge, O bacchanals, the cause divine;
Compel him with the sacred cup and rod,
To quaff his salutation to the morn,
In frothing, Massic wine!

ORPHEUS.
Mad bacchanals, begone!
I honor all the gods and Nemesis.
They favor not such frantic revelry,
But blameless lives, and deeds most like their own,
The service of a patient heart submiss,
And staunch integrity.
Behold the morning hills,
Sky-kissed Libethra, delicate as air;
The fragile grasses gray with wreaths of dew.
Hark to the tumbling of the mountain rills
To Eos and Athene your first prayer
And sacrifice are due.

BACCHANTES.
With shameless blasphemy,
He dares proscribe, O god, thy rank and fame.
Enough! enough! he hath despised us long,
Bewailing his beloved Eurydice.

O nymphs, avenge yourselves in Liber's name,
Slay him 'midst dance and song.
Your deadly javelins fling
With flinty missiles at the singer proud,
Who deems himself an equal of the gods,
Because he hath the skill to pipe and sing,
With facile fluency of speech endowed.
Smite him with spears and rods.

ORPHEUS.

Ring forth, my lyre, again,
With magic harmonies my doom avert,
In tones as plaintive and as rich as life.

BACCHANTES.

Our stones and javelins we have hurled in vain;
His lyre enchants them, he remains unhurt,
'Midst all the wrath and strife.
Toss the loud tambourine,
Its tight-drawn skin with noisy fingers smite;
Clash ye the cymbals, sing with fatal art;
Cast ye his sundered limbs the stream within,
They irritate us, soft and bare and white;
Rend them, O nymphs, apart.

ORPHEUS.

Sweet Death, deliver me
Out of the reach of envy, lust, and hate;
Enfold me in thy large-embracing arms.

BACCHANTES.

Ah! will he now invoke Eurydice,
Madly resisting his allotted fate
With vile, unhallowed charms?
So with a clamorous swell
Of drums and timbrels, we o'erpower the breath
Of dulcet and persuasive melody.

ORPHEUS.

The maniacs conquer! O my lyre, farewell!
Approach, thou beautiful and welcome Death,
With lost Eurydice.

Autumn Sadness

Air and sky are swathed in gold
Fold on fold,
Light glows through the trees like wine.
Earth, sun-quickened, swoons for bliss

'Neath his kiss,
Breathless in a trance divine.

Nature pauses from her task,
Just to bask
In these lull'd transfigured hours.
The green leaf nor stays nor goes,
But it grows
Royaler than mid-June's flowers.

Such impassioned silence fills
All the hills
Burning with unflickering fire-
Such a blood-red splendor stains
The leaves' veins,
Life seems one fulfilled desire.

While earth, sea, and heavens shine,
Heart of mine,
Say, what art thou waiting for?
Shall the cup ne'er reach the lip,
But still slip
Till the life-long thirst give o'er?

Shall my soul, no frosts may tame,
Catch new flame
From the incandescent air?
In this nuptial joy apart,
Oh my heart,
Whither shall we lonely fare?

Seek some dusky, twilight spot,
Quite forgot
Of the Autumn's Bacchic fire.
Where soft mists and shadows sleep,
There outweep
Barren longing's vain desire.

A Masque Of Venice

(A Dream.)

Not a stain,
In the sun-brimmed sapphire cup that is the sky-
Not a ripple on the black translucent lane
Of the palace-walled lagoon.
Not a cry
As the gondoliers with velvet oar glide by,
Through the golden afternoon.

From this height
Where the carved, age-yellowed balcony o'erjuts
Yonder liquid, marble pavement, see the light
Shimmer soft beneath the bridge,
That abuts
On a labyrinth of water-ways and shuts
Half their sky off with its ridge.

We shall mark
All the pageant from this ivory porch of ours,
Masques and jesters, mimes and minstrels, while we hark
To their music as they fare.
Scent their flowers
Flung from boat to boat in rainbow radiant showers
Through the laughter-ringing air.

See! they come,
Like a flock of serpent-throated black-plumed swans,
With the mandoline, viol, and the drum,
Gems afire on arms ungloved,
Fluttering fans,
Floating mantles like a great moth's streaky vans
Such as Veronese loved.

But behold
In their midst a white unruffled swan appear.
One strange barge that snowy tapestries enfold,
White its tasseled, silver prow.
Who is here?
Prince of Love in masquerade or Prince of Fear,
Clad in glittering silken snow?

Cheek and chin
Where the mask's edge stops are of the hoar-frosts hue,
And no eyebeams seem to sparkle from within
Where the hollow rings have place.
Yon gay crew
Seem to fly him, he seems ever to pursue.
'T is our sport to watch the race.

At his side
Stands the goldenest of beauties; from her glance,
From her forehead, shines the splendor of a bride,
And her feet seem shod with wings,
To entrance,
For she leaps into a wild and rhythmic dance,
Like Salome at the King's.

'T is his aim
Just to hold, to clasp her once against his breast,
Hers to flee him, to elude him in the game.

Ah, she fears him overmuch!
Is it jest,
Is it earnest? a strange riddle lurks half-guessed
In her horror of his touch.

For each time
That his snow-white fingers reach her, fades some ray
From the glory of her beauty in its prime;
And the knowledge grows upon us that the dance
Is no play
'Twixt the pale, mysterious lover and the fay
But the whirl of fate and chance.

Where the tide
Of the broad lagoon sinks plumb into the sea,
There the mystic gondolier hath won his bride.
Hark, one helpless, stifled scream!
Must it be?
Mimes and minstrels, flowers and music, where are ye?
Was all Venice such a dream?

An Epistle

I.

Master and Sage, greetings and health to thee,
From thy most meek disciple! Deign once more
Endure me at thy feet, enlighten me,
As when upon my boyish head of yore,
Midst the rapt circle gathered round thy knee
Thy sacred vials of learning thou didst pour.
By the large lustre of thy wisdom orbed
Be my black doubts illumined and absorbed.

II.

Oft I recall that golden time when thou,
Born for no second station, heldst with us
The Rabbi's chair, who art priest and bishop now;
And we, the youth of Israel, curious,
Hung on thy counsels, lifted reverent brow
Unto thy sanctity, would fain discuss
With thee our Talmud problems good and evil,
Till startled by the risen stars o'er Seville.

III.

For on the Synagogue's high-pillared porch
Thou didst hold session, till the sudden sun
Beyond day's purple limit dropped his torch.
Then we, as dreamers, woke, to find outrun

Time's rapid sands. The flame that may not scorch,
Our hearts caught from thine eyes, thou Shining One.
I scent not yet sweet lemon-groves in flower,
But I re-breathe the peace of that deep hour.

IV.

We kissed the sacred borders of thy gown,
Brow-aureoled with thy blessing, we went forth
Through the hushed byways of the twilight town.
Then in all life but one thing seemed of worth,
To seek, find, love the Truth. She set her crown
Upon thy head, our Master, at thy birth;
She bade thy lips drop honey, fired thine eyes
With the unclouded glow of sun-steeped skies.

V.

Forgive me, if I dwell on that which, viewed
From thy new vantage-ground, must seem a mist
Of error, by auroral youth endued
With alien lustre. Still in me subsist
Those reeking vapors; faith and gratitude
Still lead me to the hand my boy-lips kissed
For benison and guidance. Not in wrath,
Master, but in wise patience, point my path.

VI.

For I, thy servant, gather in one sheaf
The venomed shafts of slander, which thy word
Shall shrivel to small dust. If haply grief,
Or momentary pain, I deal, my Lord
Blame not thy servant's zeal, nor be thou deaf
Unto my soul's blind cry for light. Accord-
Pitying my love, if too superb to care
For hate-soiled name-an answer to my prayer.

VII.

To me, who, vine to stone, clung close to thee,
The very base of life appeared to quake
When first I knew thee fallen from us, to be
A tower of strength among our foes, to make
'Twixt Jew and Jew deep-cloven enmity.
I have wept gall and blood for thy dear sake.
But now with temperate soul I calmly search
Motive and cause that bound thee to the Church.

VIII.

Four motives possible therefor I reach-
Ambition, doubt, fear, or mayhap-conviction.
I hear in turn ascribed thee all and each
By ignorant folk who part not truth from fiction.
But I, whom even thyself didst stoop to teach,
May poise the scales, weigh this with that confliction,
Yea, sift the hid grain motive from the dense,
Dusty, eye-blinding chaff of consequence.

IX.

Ambition first! I find no fleck thereof
In all thy clean soul. What! could glory, gold,
Or sated senses lure thy lofty love?
No purple cloak to shield thee from the cold,
No jeweled sign to flicker thereabove,
And dazzle men to homage-joys untold
Of spiritual treasure, grace divine,
Alone (so saidst thou) coveting for thine!

X.

I saw thee mount with deprecating air,
Step after step, unto our Jewish throne
Of supreme dignity, the Rabbi's chair;
Shrinking from public honors thrust upon
Thy meek desert, regretting even there
The placid habit of thy life foregone;
Silence obscure, vast peace and austere days
Passed in wise contemplation, prayer, and praise.

XI.

One less than thou had ne'er known such regret.
How must thou suffer, who so lov'st the shade,
In Fame's full glare, whom one stride more shall set
Upon the Papal seat! I stand dismayed,
Familiar with thy fearful soul, and yet
Half glad, perceiving modest worth repaid
Even by the Christians! Could thy soul deflect?
No, no, thrice no! Ambition I reject!

XII.

Next doubt. Could doubt have swayed thee, then I ask,
How enters doubt within the soul of man?
Is it a door that opens, or a mask
That falls? and Truth's resplendent face we scan.
Nay, 't is a creeping, small, blind worm, whose task
Is gnawing at Faith's base; the whole vast plan
Rots, crumbles, eaten inch by inch within,

And on its ruins falsehood springs and sin.

XIII.

But thee no doubt confused, no problems vexed.
Thy father's faith for thee proved bright and sweet.
Thou foundst no rite superfluous, no text
Obscure; the path was straight before thy feet.
Till thy baptismal day, thou, unperplexed
By foreign dogma, didst our prayers repeat,
Honor the God of Israel, fast and feast,
Even as thy people's wont, from first to least.

XIV.

Yes, Doubt I likewise must discard. Not sleek,
Full-faced, erect of head, men walk, when doubt
Writhes at their entrails; pinched and lean of cheek,
With brow pain-branded, thou hadst strayed about
As midst live men a ghost condemned to seek
That soul he may nor live nor die without.
No doubts the font washed from thee, thou didst glide
From creed to creed, complete, sane-souled, clear-eyed.

XV.

Thy pardon, Master, if I dare sustain
The thesis thou couldst entertain a fear.
I would but rout thine enemies, who feign
Ignoble impulse prompted thy career.
I will but weigh the chances and make plain
To Envy's self the monstrous jest appear.
Though time, place, circumstance confirmed in seeming,
One word from thee should frustrate all their scheming.

XVI.

Was Israel glad in Seville on the day
Thou didst renounce him? Then mightst thou indeed
Snap finger at whate'er thy slanderers say.
Lothly must I admit, just then the seed
Of Jacob chanced upon a grievous way.
Still from the wounds of that red year we bleed.
The curse had fallen upon our heads-the sword
Was whetted for the chosen of the Lord.

XVII.

There where we flourished like a fruitful palm,
We were uprooted, spoiled, lopped limb from limb.
A bolt undreamed of out of heavens calm,

So cracked our doom. We were destroyed by him
Whose hand since childhood we had clasped. With balm
Our head had been anointed, at the brim
Our cup ran over-now our day was done,
Our blood flowed free as water in the sun.

XVIII.

Midst the four thousand of our tribe who held
Glad homes in Seville, never a one was spared,
Some slaughtered at their hearthstones, some expelled
To Moorish slavery. Cunningly ensnared,
Baited and trapped were we; their fierce monks yelled
And thundered from our Synagogues, while flared
The Cross above the Ark. Ah, happiest they
Who fell unconquered martyrs on that day!

XIX.

For some (I write it with flushed cheek, bowed head),
Given free choice 'twixt death and shame, chose shame,
Denied the God who visibly had led
Their fathers, pillared in a cloud of flame,
Bathed in baptismal waters, ate the bread
Which is their new Lord's body, took the name
Marranos the Accursed, whom equally
Jew, Moor, and Christian hate, despise, and flee.

XX.

Even one no less than an Abarbanel
Prized miserable length of days, above
Integrity of soul. Midst such who fell,
Far be it, however, from my duteous love,
Master, to reckon thee. Thine own lips tell
How fear nor torture thy firm will could move.
How thou midst panic nowise disconcerted,
By Thomas of Aquinas wast converted!

XXI.

Truly I know no more convincing way
To read so wise an author, than was thine.
When burning Synagogues changed night to day,
And red swords underscored each word and line.
That was a light to read by! Who'd gainsay
Authority so clearly stamped divine?
On this side, death and torture, flame and slaughter,
On that, a harmless wafer and clean water.

XXII.

Thou couldst not fear extinction for our race;
Though Christian sword and fire from town to town
Flash double bladed lightning to efface
Israel's image-though we bleed, burn, drown
Through Christendom-'t is but a scanty space.
Still are the Asian hills and plains our own,
Still are we lords in Syria, still are free,
Nor doomed to be abolished utterly.

XXIII.

One sole conclusion hence at last I find,
Thou whom ambition, doubt, nor fear could swerve,
Perforce hast been persuaded through the mind,
Proved, tested the new dogmas, found them serve
Thy spirit's needs, left flesh and sense behind,
Accepted without shrinking or reserve,
The trans-substantial bread and wine, the Christ
At whose shrine thine own kin were sacrificed.

XXIV.

Here then the moment comes when I crave light.
All's dark to me. Master, if I be blind,
Thou shalt unseal my lids and bless with sight,
Or groping in the shadows, I shall find
Whether within me or without, dwell night.
Oh cast upon my doubt-bewildered mind
One ray from thy clear heaven of sun-bright faith,
Grieving, not wroth, at what thy servant saith.

XXV.

Where are the signs fulfilled whereby all men
Should know the Christ? Where is the wide-winged peace
Shielding the lamb within the lion's den?
The freedom broadening with the wars that cease?
Do foes clasp hands in brotherhood again?
Where is the promised garden of increase,
When like a rose the wilderness should bloom?
Earth is a battlefield and Spain a tomb.

XXVI.

Our God of Sabaoth is an awful God
Of lightnings and of vengeance,-Christians say.
Earth trembled, nations perished at his nod;
His Law has yielded to a milder sway.
Theirs is the God of Love whose feet have trod
Our common earth-draw near to him and pray,

Meek-faced, dove-eyed, pure-browed, the Lord of life,
Know him and kneel, else at your throat the knife!

XXVII.

This is the God of Love, whose altars reek
With human blood, who teaches men to hate;
Torture past words, or sins we may not speak
Wrought by his priests behind the convent-grate.
Are his priests false? or are his doctrines weak
That none obeys him? State at war with state,
Church against church-yea, Pope at feud with Pope
In these tossed seas what anchorage for hope?

XXVIII.

Not only for the sheep without the fold
Is the knife whetted, who refuse to share
Blessings the shepherd wise doth not withhold
Even from the least among his flock-but there
Midmost the pale, dissensions manifold,
Lamb flaying lamb, fierce sheep that rend and tear.
Master, if thou to thy pride's goal should come,
Where wouldst thou throne-at Avignon or Rome?

XXIX.

I handle burning questions, good my lord,
Such as may kindle fagots, well I wis.
Your Gospel not denies our older Word,
But in a way completes and betters this.
The Law of Love shall supersede the sword,
So runs the promise, but the facts I miss.
Already needs this wretched generation,
A voice divine-a new, third revelation.

XXX.

Two Popes and their adherents fulminate
Ban against ban, and to the nether hell
Condemn each other, while the nations wait
Their Christ to thunder forth from Heaven, and tell
Who is his rightful Vicar, reinstate
His throne, the hideous discord to dispel.
Where shall I seek, master, while such things be,
Celestial truth, revealed certainty!

XXXI.

Not miracles I doubt, for how dare man,
Chief miracle of life's mystery, say HE KNOWS?

How may he closely secret causes scan,
Who learns not whence he comes nor where he goes?
Like one who walks in sleep a doubtful span
He gropes through all his days, till Death unclose
His cheated eyes and in one blinding gleam,
Wakes, to discern the substance from the dream.

XXXII.

I say not therefore I deny the birth,
The Virgin's motherhood, the resurrection,
Who know not how mine own soul came to earth,
Nor what shall follow death. Man's imperfection
May bound not even in thought the height and girth
Of God's omnipotence; neath his direction
We may approach his essence, but that He
Should dwarf Himself to us-it cannot be!

XXXIII.

The God who balances the clouds, who spread
The sky above us like a molten glass,
The God who shut the sea with doors, who laid
The corner-stone of earth, who caused the grass
Spring forth upon the wilderness, and made
The darkness scatter and the night to pass-
That He should clothe Himself with flesh, and move
Midst worms a worm-this, sun, moon, stars disprove.

XXXIV.

Help me, O thou who wast my boyhood's guide,
I bend my exile-weary feet to thee,
Teach me the indivisible to divide,
Show me how three are one and One is three!
How Christ to save all men was crucified,
Yet I and mine are damned eternally.
Instruct me, Sage, why Virtue starves alone,
While falsehood step by step ascends the throne.

The Feast Of Lights

Kindle the taper like the steadfast star
Ablaze on evening's forehead o'er the earth,
And add each night a lustre till afar
An eightfold splendor shine above thy hearth.
Clash, Israel, the cymbals, touch the lyre,
Blow the brass trumpet and the harsh-tongued horn;
Chant psalms of victory till the heart takes fire,

The Maccabean spirit leap new-born.

Remember how from wintry dawn till night,
Such songs were sung in Zion, when again
On the high altar flamed the sacred light,
And, purified from every Syrian stain,
The foam-white walls with golden shields were hung,
With crowns and silken spoils, and at the shrine,
Stood, midst their conqueror-tribe, five chieftains sprung
From one heroic stock, one seed divine.

Five branches grown from Mattathias' stem,
The Blessed John, the Keen-Eyed Jonathan,
Simon the fair, the Burst-of Spring, the Gem,
Eleazar, Help of-God; o'er all his clan
Judas the Lion-Prince, the Avenging Rod,
Towered in warrior-beauty, uncrowned king,
Armed with the breastplate and the sword of God,
Whose praise is: 'He received the perishing.'

They who had camped within the mountain-pass,
Couched on the rock, and tented neath the sky,
Who saw from Mizpah's heights the tangled grass
Choke the wide Temple-courts, the altar lie
Disfigured and polluted-who had flung
Their faces on the stones, and mourned aloud
And rent their garments, wailing with one tongue,
Crushed as a wind-swept bed of reeds is bowed,

Even they by one voice fired, one heart of flame,
Though broken reeds, had risen, and were men,
They rushed upon the spoiler and o'ercame,
Each arm for freedom had the strength of ten.
Now is their mourning into dancing turned,
Their sackcloth doffed for garments of delight,
Week-long the festive torches shall be burned,
Music and revelry wed day with night.

Still ours the dance, the feast, the glorious Psalm,
The mystic lights of emblem, and the Word.
Where is our Judas? Where our five-branched palm?
Where are the lion-warriors of the Lord?
Clash, Israel, the cymbals, touch the lyre,
Sound the brass trumpet and the harsh-tongued horn,
Chant hymns of victory till the heart take fire,
The Maccabean spirit leap new-born!

In Memoriam

O friend who passed away while flowers died,
Now that the land bursts into bloom again,
With vivid blossoms o'er the landscape wide,
Purple and white 'mongst, grasses golden-eyed,
In beauteous resurrection o'er the plain,

My thoughts revert to thee, who liest still,
Under the pulsing, stirring, glowing earth;
Not rising with the lilac on the hill,
Not waking with the sunny daffodil,
Living and breathing with no second birth.

In these sweet days I dream I see thy grave,
A mockery of death, alive with flowers.
The delicate sprays and tender grasses wave,
Blue violets and the hardy crocus brave,
Wooed back to life by sunshine, dew, and showers.

I cannot deem that thou art lying there,
Asleep through all these fervent days of spring;
For I perceive thy spirit in the air,
Around me ever in my dream and prayer,
Enskied and hallowed by thy suffering.

When thou didst walk upon the earth before,
My trivial words and deeds alone were thine;
But now my holiest dreams are evermore
Blended with thoughts of thee, on that far shore,
Where thy pale, girlish face has grown divine.

Through the dark shadows thou must go alone;
And lo! thou hast a dauntless bravery,
A most majestic resignation shown;
A valiant patience, a faith not overthrown
By the dread terror of uncertainty.

The day had fled, from thee for evermore,
Thy soul was ebbing with the waning light,
And still thou asked, aweary and heartsore,
The same pathetic question o'er and o'er,
'O, I am tired! will I go to-night?'

Aye, thou didst go, and where? Thou knowest now.
Nature is innocent as well as fair;
Lillies, as well as amaranth, wreathe her brow.
She hath thy soul; because I cannot know
Where it may be, I feel it everywhere.

And thus the spring hath brought me flowers of worth.
O mourners, cease to weep o'er empty graves!
Open them all! no dead come trooping forth,

To fill with ghastly hosts the living earth;
Only the flowers bloom, the green grass waves.

Those ye laid low with solemn rites and tears,
Elude you; while ye weep, they all have flown.
And so I lay aside my doubts and fears;
My friend in day-dreams and at night appears,
And hovers near when I am most alone.

Idyl

The swallows made twitter incessant,
The thrushes were wild with their mirth.
The ways and the woods were made pleasant,
And the flowering nooks of the earth.
And the sunshine sufficed to rejoice me,
And the air was as bracing as wine,
And the sky and the shadows and grasses
Were enough to make living divine.

Then I saw on the ground two gray robins,
One with glorious flame-colored vest,
'Neath the shade of some delicate bluebells,
By the breeze of the morning caressed.
They were singing of love in the shadow;
She was bashful, and modest, and coy,
And he sang to her tenderest love-songs,
And madrigals full of his joy.

And his song came forth clearer and clearer,
With each passionate, musical note;
Like the ripple of silvery waters,
It gushed from his beautiful throat.
His whole little bird-soul he offers,
Ah! she listens to him as he sings:
Then he ceases, awaiting her answer,
With bright eyes and with quivering wings.

And I, too, stood awaiting it, breathless,
For his song was too sweet to disdain,
Till it came, little notes full of gladness,
With a plaintive and tender refrain.
And the songs died away in the distance,
And the forest alone heard the rest,
As the two little lovers flew upward,
To build them together a nest.

Niagara

Thou art a giant altar, where the Earth
Must needs send up her thanks to Him above
Who did create her. Nature cometh here
To lay its offerings upon thy shrine.
The morning and the evening shower down
Bright jewels, changeful opals, em'ralds fair.
The burning noon sends floods of molten gold,
The calm night crowns thee with its host of stars,
The moon enfolds thee with her silver veil,
And o'er thee e'er is arched the rainbow's span,
The gorgeous marriage-ring of Earth and Heaven.
While ever from the holy altar grand
Ascends the incense of the mist and spray,
That mounts to God with thy wild roar of praise

Wings

Dawn opes her pensive eyes,
In the yet starry skies,
A roseate blush upon her cheek and brows.
Her purple mantle still
Lies on the sky-kissed hill,
And a blue, solemn shade thereon it throws.

The earth lies hushed and calm.
No chant of praise, no psalm
Riseth to greet the rose-crowned queen of day.
Each blade of grass, each leaf,
Stands out in sharp relief,
Against the rayless blue and silver gray.

All nature seems to wait
For some new deed of Fate;
The silence is a sacred, reverent prayer,
When hark! from some sweet throat
One thrilling, quivering note
Fills with its tremulous music all the air.

Then from the dewy grass
A tiny form doth pass,
A little soul all music and all wings.
All nature's voice is heard,
Embodied in this bird,
That darteth up and, rising, ever sings.

It mounteth still and sings:
What soul yearns not for wings,

To follow after, burst its prison bars,
And learn the secret there,
In those clear realms of air,
The secret of the rainbow and the stars;

To rush as swift as light,
Within those regions bright
Of throbbing, scintillant, intensest blue;
The air all breathless cleave,
And far below to leave
Regrets and tears, the raindrop and the dew.

Ah! caged 'mongst meaner things,
The soul can use no wings,
And beats against the bars it cannot pass;
But it might humbly turn,
Essaying first to learn
The secret of the flowers and the grass.

The Day Of Dead Soldiers

Welcome, thou gray and fragrant Sabbath-day,
To deathless love and valor dedicate!
Glorious with the richest flowers of May,
With early roses, lingering lilacs late,
With vivid green of grass and leaf and spray,
Thou bringest memories that far outweigh
The season's joy with thoughts of death and fate.

What words may paint the picture on the air
Of this broad land to-day from sea to sea?
The rolling prairies, purple valleys rare,
And royal mountains, endless rivers free,
Filled full with phantoms flitting everywhere,
Pale ghosts of buried armies, slowly there
From countless graves uprising silently.

A calm, grave day,—the sunlight does not shine
But thin, gray clouds bedrape the sky o'erhead.
The delicate air is filled with spirits fine,
The temperate breezes whisper of the dead.
What visions and what memories divine,
O holy Sabbath flower-day, are thine,
Painted in light against a field of red!

Behold the fairest spots in all the land,
To-day in this mid-season of fresh flowers,
Are heroes' graves, by many a tender hand
Sprinkled With odorous, radiant-colored showers;

By mild, moist breezes delicately fanned,
Sending o'er distant towns their perfumes bland,
Loading with sweet aroma sunless hours.

Who knows what tremulous, dusky hands set free,
Deck quaintly with gay flowers the graves unknown?
What wealth of bloom is shed exuberantly,
On the far grave in Illinois alone,
Where the last hero, sleeping peacefully,
Beyond detraction and mistrust, doth lie,
By the glad winds of prairies overblown?

With hymns and prayer be this day sanctified,
And consecrate to heroes' memories;
Not with wild, violent grief for those who died,
O wives and mothers, but with patience wise,
Calm resignation, and a thankful pride,
That they have left their land a fame so wide,
So rich a page of thrilling histories.

Agamemnon's Tomb

Uplift the ponderous, golden mask of death,
And let the sun shine on him as it did
How many thousand years agone! Beneath
This worm-defying, uncorrupted lid,
Behold the young, heroic face, round-eyed,
Of one who in his full-flowered manhood died;
Of nobler frame than creatures of to-day,
Swathed in fine linen cerecloths fold on fold,
With carven weapons wrought of bronze and gold,
Accoutred like a warrior for the fray.

We gaze in awe at these huge-modeled limbs,
Shrunk in death's narrow house, but hinting yet
Their ancient majesty; these sightless rims
Whose living eyes the eyes of Helen met;
The speechless lips that ah! what tales might tell
Of earth's morning-tide when gods did dwell
Amidst a generous-fashioned, god-like race,
Who dwarf our puny semblance, and who won
The secret soul of Beauty for their own,
While all our art but crudely apes their grace.

We gather all the precious relics up,
The golden buttons chased with wondrous craft,
The sculptured trinkets and the crystal cup,
The sheathed, bronze sword, the knife with brazen haft.
Fain would we wrest with curious eyes from these

Unnumbered long-forgotten histories,
The deeds heroic of this mighty man,
On whom once more the living daylight beams,
To shame our littleness, to mock our dreams,
And the abyss of centuries to span.

Yet could we rouse him from his blind repose,
How might we meet his searching questionings,
Concerning all the follies, wrongs, and woes,
Since his great day whom men call King of Kings,
Victorious Agamemnon? How might we
Those large, clear eyes confront, which scornfully
Would view us as a poor, degenerate race,
Base-souled and mean-proportioned? What reply
Give to the beauty-loving Greek's heart-cry,
Seeking his ancient gods in vacant space?

What should he find within a world grown cold,
Save doubt and trouble? To his sunny creed
A thousand gloomy, warring sects succeed.
How of the Prince of Peace might he be told,
When over half the world the war-cloud lowers?
How would he mock these faltering hopes of ours,
Who knows the secret now of death and fate!
Humbly we gaze on the colossal frame,
And mutely we accept the mortal shame,
Of men degraded from a high estate.

In A Swedish Graveyard

After wearisome toil and much sorrow,
How quietly sleep they at last,
Neither dreading and fearing the morrow,
Nor vainly bemoaning the past!
Shall we give them our envy or pity?
Shall we shun or yearn after such rest,
So calm near the turbulent city,
With their heart stilled at length in their breast?

They all sleep with their heads lying westward,
Where all suns and all days have gone down.
Do they long for the dawn, looking eastward?
Do they dream of the strife and the crown?
Each one held a lit taper when dying:
Where hath vanished the fugitive flame?
With his love, and his joy, and his sighing,
Alas! and his youth and his name.

The living stands o'er him and dreameth,

And wonders what dreams came to him.
While the tender, brief twilight still gleameth,
With a light strangely mournful and dim.
And he wonders what lights and what shadows
Passed over these dead long ago,
When their feet now at rest trod these meadows,
And their hearts throbbed to pleasure or woe

What dreams came to them in their living?
The self-same that come now to thee.
If thou findest those dreams are deceiving,
Then these lives thou wilt know and wilt see:
The same visions of love and of glory,
The same vain regret for the past;
All the same poor and pitiful story,
Till the taper's extinguished at last.

All the treasures on earth that they cherished,
Now they care not to clasp nor to save;
And the poor little lights, how they perished,
Slowly dying alone in the grave!
With a flickering faint on the features
Of age, or of youth in its bloom:
Lighting up for grim Death his weak creatures,
In the darkness and night of the tomb,

With a radiance ghostly and mournful,
On the good, on the just and unjust;
For a space, till the monarch, so scornful,
Turned the light and the lighted to dust.
No taper of earth he desired
In his halls where they quietly rest;
For all those who have toiled and are tired,
Utter darkness and sleep may be best.

Off Rough Point

We sat at twilight nigh the sea,
The fog hung gray and weird.
Through the thick film uncannily
The broken moon appeared.

We heard the billows crack and plunge,
We saw nor waves nor ships.
Earth sucked the vapors like a sponge,
The salt spray wet our lips.

Closer the woof of white mist drew,
Before, behind, beside.

How could that phantom moon break through,
Above that shrouded tide?

The roaring waters filled the ear,
A white blank foiled the sight.
Close-gathering shadows near, more near,
Brought the blind, awful night.

O friends who passed unseen, unknown!
O dashing, troubled sea!
Still stand we on a rock alone,
Walled round by mystery.

On A Tuft Of Grass

Weak, slender blades of tender green,
With little fragrance, little sheen,
What maketh ye so dear to all?
Nor bud, nor flower, nor fruit have ye,
So tiny, it can only be
'Mongst fairies ye are counted tall.

No beauty is in this, ah, yea,
E'en as I gaze on you to-day,
Your hue and fragrance bear me back
Into the green, wide fields of old,
With clear, blue air, and manifold
Bright buds and flowers in blossoming track.

All bent one way like flickering flame,
Each blade caught sunlight as it came,
Then rising, saddened into shade;
A changeful, wavy, harmless sea,
Whose billows none could bitterly
Reproach with wrecks that they had made.

No gold ever was buried there
More rich, more precious, or more fair
Than buttercups with yellow gloss.
No ships of mighty forest trees
E'er foundered in these guiltless seas
Of grassy waves and tender moss.

Ah, no! ah, no! not guiltless still,
Green waves on meadow and on hill,
Not wholly innocent are ye;
For what dead hopes and loves, what graves,
Lie underneath your placid waves,
While breezes kiss them lovingly!

Calm sleepers with sealed eyes lie there;
They see not, neither feel nor care
If over them the grass be green.
And some sleep here who ne'er knew rest,
Until the grass grew o'er their breast,
And stilled the aching pain within.

Not all the sorrow man hath known,
Not all the evil he hath done,
Have ever cast thereon a stain.
It groweth green and fresh and light,
As in the olden garden bright,
Beneath the feet of Eve and Cain.

It flutters, bows, and bends, and quivers,
And creeps through forests and by rivers,
Each blade with dewy brightness wet,
So soft, so quiet, and so fair,
We almost dream of sleeping there,
Without or sorrow or regret.

Restlessness

Would I had waked this morn where Florence smiles,
A-bloom with beauty, a white rose full-blown,
Yet rich in sacred dust, in storied stone,
Precious past all the wealth of Indian isles-
From olive-hoary Fiesole to feed
On Brunelleschi's dome my hungry eye,
And see against the lotus-colored sky,
Spring the slim belfry graceful as a reed.
To kneel upon the ground where Dante trod,
To breathe the air of immortality
From Angelo and Raphael-TO BE-
Each sense new-quickened by a demi-god.
To hear the liquid Tuscan speech at whiles,
From citizen and peasant, to behold
The heaven of Leonardo washed with gold-
Would I had waked this morn where Florence smile!

On The Proposal To Erect A Monument In England To Lord Byron Poem

The grass of fifty Aprils hath waved green
Above the spent heart, the Olympian head,
The hands crost idly, the shut eyes unseen,
Unseeing, the locked lips whose song hath fled;

Yet mystic-lived, like some rich, tropic flower,
His fame puts forth fresh blossoms hour by hour;
Wide spread the laden branches dropping dew
On the low, laureled brow misunderstood,
That bent not, neither bowed, until subdued
By the last foe who crowned while he o'erthrew.

Fair was the Easter Sabbath morn when first
Men heard he had not wakened to its light:
The end had come, and time had done its worst,
For the black cloud had fallen of endless night.
Then in the town, as Greek accosted Greek,
'T was not the wonted festal words to speak,
'Christ is arisen,' but 'Our chief is gone,'
With such wan aspect and grief-smitten head
As when the awful cry of 'Pan is dead!'
Filled echoing hill and valley with its moan.

'I am more fit for death than the world deems,'
So spake he as life's light was growing dim,
And turned to sleep as unto soothing dreams.
What terrors could its darkness hold for him,
Familiar with all anguish, but with fear
Still unacquainted? On his martial bier
They laid a sword, a helmet, and a crown-
Meed of the warrior, but not these among
His voiceless lyre, whose silent chords unstrung
Shall wait-how long?-for touches like his own.

An alien country mourned him as her son,
And hailed him hero: his sole, fitting tomb
Were Theseus' temple or the Parthenon,
Fondly she deemed. His brethren bare him home,
Their exiled glory, past the guarded gate
Where England's Abbey shelters England's great.
Afar he rests whose very name hath shed
New lustre on her with the song he sings.
So Shakespeare rests who scorned to lie with kings,
Sleeping at peace midst the unhonored dead.

And fifty years suffice to overgrow
With gentle memories the foul weeds of hate
That shamed his grave. The world begins to know
Her loss, and view with other eyes his fate.
Even as the cunning workman brings to pass
The sculptor's thought from out the unwieldy mass
Of shapeless marble, so Time lops away
The stony crust of falsehood that concealed
His just proportions, and, at last revealed,
The statue issues to the light of day,

Most beautiful, most human. Let them fling
The first stone who are tempted even as he,
And have not swerved. When did that rare soul sing
The victim's shame, the tyrant's eulogy,
The great belittle, or exalt the small,
Or grudge his gift, his blood, to disenthrall
The slaves of tyranny or ignorance?
Stung by fierce tongues himself, whose rightful fame
Hath he reviled? Upon what noble name
Did the winged arrows of the barbed wit glance?

The years' thick, clinging curtains backward pull,
And show him as he is, crowned with bright beams,
'Beauteous, and yet not all as beautiful
As he hath been or might be; Sorrow seems
Half of his immortality.' He needs
No monument whose name and song and deeds
Are graven in all foreign hearts; but she
His mother, England, slow and last to wake,
Needs raise the votive shaft for her fame's sake:
Hers is the shame if such forgotten be!

Reality

These things alone endure;
'They are the solid facts,' that we may grasp,
Leading us on and upward if we clasp
And hold them firm and sure.

In a wise fable old,
A hero sought a god who could at will
Assume all figures, and the hero still
Loosed not his steadfast hold,

For image foul or fair,
For soft-eyed nymph, who wept with pain and shame,
For threatening fiend or loathsome beast or flame,
For menace or for prayer.

Until the god, outbraved,
Took his own shape divine; not wrathfully,
But wondering, to the hero gave reply,
The knowledge that he craved.

We seize the god in youth;
All forms conspire to make us loose our grasp,
Ambition, folly, gain, till we unclasp
From the embrace of truth.

We grow more wise, we say,
And work for worldly ends and mock our dream,
Alas! while all life's glory and its gleam,
With that have fled away.

If thereto we had clung
Through change and peril, fire and night and storm,
Till it assumed its proper, godlike form,
We might at last have wrung

An answer to our cries
A brave response to our most valiant hope.
Unto the light of day this word might ope
A million mysteries.

O'er each man's brow I see
The bright star of his genius shining clear;
It seeks to guide him to a nobler sphere,
Above earth's vanity.

Up to pure height of snow,
Its beckoning ray still leads him on and on;
To those who follow, lo, itself comes down
And crowns at length their brow.

The nimbus still doth gleam
On these the heroes, sages of the earth,
The few who found, in life of any worth,
Only their loftiest dream.

In Exile

Twilight is here, soft breezes bow the grass,
Day's sounds of various toil break slowly off,
The yoke-freed oxen low, the patient ass
Dips his dry nostril in the cool, deep trough.
Up from the prairie the tanned herdsmen pass
With frothy pails, guiding with voices rough
Their udder-lightened kine. Fresh smells of earth,
The rich, black furrows of the glebe send forth.

After the Southern day of heavy toil,
How good to lie, with limbs relaxed, brows bare
To evening's fan, and watch the smoke-wreaths coil
Up from one's pipe-stem through the rayless air.
So deem these unused tillers of the soil,
Who stretched beneath the shadowing oak tree, stare
Peacefully on the star-unfolding skies,
And name their life unbroken paradise.

The hounded stag that has escaped the pack,
And pants at ease within a thick-leaved dell;
The unimprisoned bird that finds the track
Through sun-bathed space, to where his fellows dwell;
The martyr, granted respite from the rack,
The death-doomed victim pardoned from his cell,
Such only know the joy these exiles gain,
Life's sharpest rapture is surcease of pain.

Strange faces theirs, wherethrough the Orient sun
Gleams from the eyes and glows athwart the skin.
Grave lines of studious thought and purpose run
From curl-crowned forehead to dark-bearded chin.
And over all the seal is stamped thereon
Of anguish branded by a world of sin,
In fire and blood through ages on their name,
Their seal of glory and the Gentiles' shame.

Freedom to love the law that Moses brought,
To sing the songs of David, and to think
The thoughts Gabirol to Spinoza taught,
Freedom to dig the common earth, to drink
The universal air-for this they sought
Refuge o'er wave and continent, to link
Egypt with Texas in their mystic chain,
And truth's perpetual lamp forbid to wane.

Hark! through the quiet evening air, their song
Floats forth with wild sweet rhythm and glad refrain.
They sing the conquest of the spirit strong,
The soul that wrests the victory from pain;
The noble joys of manhood that belong
To comrades and to brothers. In their strain
Rustle of palms and Eastern streams one hears,
And the broad prairie melts in mist of tears.